#CompletelySingle

Learning How to Become the Right ONE Before Meeting the Right One

by Damien K. H. Nash

Also By Damien K. H. Nash

How to Load Your Truck: The 4 Keys to Discovering Your Potential, 2nd Edition

Thoughts From The Box: 31 Day Devotional

Big Box, Little Box: How One Little Box Finds His Way

Big Box, Little Box: The Forecast Calls For Potential Rain!

Gift Presented

To

_____

From

_____

Date

_____

#Completely Single

Learning How to Become the Right ONE Before Meeting the Right One

by Damien K. H. Nash

An imprint of TNG Publishings, LLC. We Deliver Potential. ® www.tngpublishings.com

#Completely Single: Learning How to Become the Right One Before Meeting the Right One

First published by TNG Publishings, LLC

ISBN 978-1512142082

Printed in the United States of America. This book is printed on acid-free paper.

publishings

P.O. Box 81011 Conyers, GA 30013 info@tngpublishings.com www.tngpublishings.com

Ordering Information: Quantity sales. Special discounts are available to corporations, associations, and others on quantity purchases. For details, contact the publisher at the address above.

This book is dedicated to my Fusion Church Family.

– Damien

Table of Contents

Foreword

Two words: *Completely Single*. Wow ... I will start out by saying this: my good friend Damien Nash has hit this one over the fence and to the upper deck! Honestly. At first, I thought there was nothing more to know about relationships and being single. I thought everything had been made public already through magazine articles and other self-help books. But that was until Jesus got a hold of a young man and gave him a fresh, God-inspired word. Not only are Damien and I good friends, but for years now we have also been each other's accountability partner, privileged to speak correction and encouragement into one another's life.

So much is touched on throughout this incredibly authentic book. By hitting the delete button on those nagging single-life issues, an individual can make for a blessed married-life. Speaking from personal experience, being married for only a few years now myself (to a beautiful, wonderful, godly woman), I can see in my own marriage numerous stumbling blocks that Damien speaks of. Even though I deleted many of the same issues I knew would be detrimental, several have exposed themselves in my marriage. This brings up the question: How completely single was I? Only God knows that answer ... and only God knows that answer concerning you. While you are developing your purpose, identity, and direction in Christ, analyze your life through prayer and see what needs to **go** so that you can **grow**. Erasing what the world has taught you is one key. Establishing the powerful points made in this book is the other.

Do yourself this favor: Die to the things that are killing you and keeping you from wholeness. Secondly, live for the things that are reviving you and making you whole. "Live by faith and walk with wisdom" is my favorite line. Damien and I are walking this dirt road of life with you. Never forget it.

My inspiration and my motivation is this: Die so that you may live! Live so that others may know you are truly alive! Become *#CompletelySingle*!

– Justin Hart

It is not just an opinion, but also a fact that Damien is a good friend to my husband. His spiritual walk shines through in many aspects, whether it be in his daily conversations or in his written work. This book, *#CompletelySingle*, is something bigger than himself. I see Damien striving to become whole in Christ, and as he is doing so, he is bringing others with him. That is probably one of his best qualities: unselfish boldness. He shares with others what God teaches him and does not keep it locked within himself. The topics discussed in this book are candid and refreshing. His personal stories hit home. His insight is coming from an angle that most male and female believers have never read before. The world will learn countless things about our friend in this unique relationship book; but perhaps, more than that, they will learn even more about themselves and their relationship with Christ. Without God, we **all** are incomplete while single. Yet with Him, we all can be complete and whole, lacking nothing. Enjoy the book…

– *Jasmine Hart*

Introduction

Tackling Loneliness

One night at work I was meditating on the word *relationships*. I work the midnight shift in the corporate office of one of the most prestigious airline companies in the world. You see, so many young adults in my church community were struggling with this subject of relationships. If you knew me, you would know I love to solve problems and come up with solutions to help people struggling in any area of their life. I am finding out that every area in which we struggle with has a biblical answer to it. So I decided to listen to God to help me apply this wisdom to my own life first and then share it with those around me.

I asked the Spirit of God to direct me in this search, to give me something that was uncanny and transforming—something I personally had never heard before that would not just be a word to itch the ears of the listeners, but would also transform lives for generations.

Then I felt the Spirit say, "If you want to know about relationships, look at the first relationship." I thought about it some more and I said, "Well, the first relationship was with You and Adam." Man, so I pulled up the Bible electronically at work, and I started seeing where

God was going with this. After receiving five of the six principles found in Genesis 2—which form the basis for this book—I literally had to contain myself from turning over my computer screens. Those who know me know that I am *so* serious about that.

I then started messaging my close friends over the next couple of days, showing them what God had given me about relationships. Their excitement made me more excited! The sixth principle came when I was going over it again with my sis' Jasmine Hart—as she pointed out a verse that I had overlooked.

I know you are wondering why I am writing a book like this. What was my inspiration for this work? Well, as I served as a prayer team leader at my current church, I continued to hear some of the same prayers being prayed over and over again. Most of the time my team members prayed about what they were currently going through—until I taught them biblical principles on how to be less defensive and more assertive in praying. We would have prayers like "Lord, help me get over this guy" or "Help me let go of this girl."

Also, what I continued to see is that relationships were the major topics of prayers, but these same people still were not successful in relationships after they prayed. Where was the disconnect? We sometimes think that just letting the person go will make us single again so we can find Mr./Mrs. right. What you will learn in this book is that this is the furthest from the truth. There might be remnants of past relationships that affect your perspective in a future relationship if you don't address those soul-ties, which are strongholds you need to overcome.

So before I go any further in this book, I want to make a foundational statement: **The most important relationship is man's relationship with God.** The success or destruction of humanity hinges on our relationship with God. Once our relationship with God is back in order, we will start seeing real and lasting changes in our human relationships.

I truly believe that this principle, when applied, will radically change your life and your views to focus on being completely single as you enter into relationships. Now, I know this does not sound attractive at this time; however, bear with me as I take you through what I believe God intended in establishing our first healthy relationship, which should be with Him.

That said, God intends us to cultivate relationships with other people as well. I love Ecclesiastes 4:9–12:

> *Two are better than one, because they have a good*

*return for their labor: If either of them falls down, one can help the other up. But pity anyone who falls and has no one to help them up. Also, if two lie down together, they will keep warm. But how can one keep warm **alone**. Though one may be over-powered, two can defend themselves. A cord of three strands is not quickly broken.* (NIV)

This is not a book that invokes the modern-day termi-nology floating around, like "the gift of singleness." As I have studied the word, I don't see singleness so much as a gift but a choice. What I can say is that God knows what is best for each of us. He says in Genesis 2:18, "*It is not good for the man to be alone…*" (NIV).

In the Hebrew, *alone* takes on a couple of meanings like "All-one" or "All-in-One." God's plan was not to keep man "all-in-one". We read in Genesis 2:21 that He created a female and actually pulled her out of man by opening him up. Man left by himself will self-de-struct—and the enemy wants us to self-destruct. We sometimes isolate ourselves, detached and cut off from friends, brothers and sisters, and our families. We play right into the enemies' plan for our lives.

However, God wanted to create a system that would fight against the enemy's future schemes of isolation: reproduction. God didn't want to continue to pull humans out of man, so he created "Womb-man," known to us as *woman*.

So to those who may think their current situation as single is a death sentence, let me tell you: the enemy wants to deceive your mind, saying that you are alone or all-in-one. You see, God has a plan for that. Yes, you might not have a courtship partner or spouse in your life currently, but that does not mean you are alone. Deuteronomy 31:6 says, *"Be strong and courageous. Do not be afraid or terrified because of them, for the Lord your God goes with you; he will never leave you nor forsake you"* (NIV).

That's right. No matter what fight you are in, whether the fight against the enemy or the internal fights in your mind, you have to remember He will never leave you nor forsake you. God is with you, and He loves you!

Let me tell you a brief story. One day at a family meeting, my older brother David said something that changed my life. You see, I was struggling with a bout of loneliness again as I was trying to realize God's purpose for my life. I say "again" because my struggle with this almost cost me my life in college. My brother saw that I lacked true friendship even though my life was filled with people. He said, "If you want friends, be friendly." This is such a simple phrase, but it is also profound.

I'm an introvert; however, I had to learn that I was making choices to stay introverted. As followers of Christ, we have to recognize that we can't blame our personality traits for our loneliness. We can seek God's guidance to help us be a light for Him. It's our choice! He gave us free will. One thing I have found in my journey was that even though I was single, I was never alone—because God was there. As I mentioned before, I made a decision to surround myself with people who hold me accountable. These are people who sharpen me to be the person God has called me to be while helping me to vanquish loneliness and isolation.

There are several ways I approached this study on reasons for loneliness. I wanted this introduction to help give you a process to tackle loneliness whenever you might have these feelings. Dr. David Jeremiah contributed to the concepts behind these four steps through his teachings entitled Slaying the Giant of Loneliness:

1. First you must accept or admit that you are lonely. Consider the causes of your loneliness. Let's be honest, we all have had this feeling at some point in our lives. So what things are out there that may cause our loneliness? For starters: sickness, big dreams or visions, death, unrealistic expectations, phobias, sin, depression, moving from place to place, social media, and relationships or the lack thereof. I encourage you to talk to someone about your feelings and acknowledge that these feelings are real!

2. The second step we should take is to accept our provision for loneliness. Jesus knew that it was better for Him to leave so He could send help that would be accessible to each of us simultaneously. In John 14:16 Jesus tells us exactly where that help is coming from: *"And I will ask the Father, and he will give you another advocate to help you and be with you forever"* (NIV). He has given us His Holy Spirit, who is known as "the Comforter" and "our Help." We just need to stand on these promises in Scripture when moments of loneliness start rising inside of us, and believe that He will be there for us forever.

3. C. S. Lewis's wife Joy Davidman died in 1960, and Lewis was very distraught. Yes, it was sad that she died, but it was recorded that he was more upset at himself because every day after her death, he was losing her image in his mind. I believe the reason why so many people are lonely is because they continue to lose the very image of Christ. They sometimes lack the discipline to spend time with Him by reading His word or even praying often. **Spend time often in reading the**

Word of God so you can regain the image of Christ upon your heart. In the Bible you may run across Hebrews 13:5: *"Keep your lives free from the love of money and be content with what you have, because God has said, 'Never will I leave you; never will I forsake you'"* (NIV).

One of the things I also learned during my study is that Jesus became lonely on a cross so we would never be lonely. We read about His loneliness in the prophecy of Isaiah 53:3a, which says, *"He was despised and rejected by mankind, a man of suffering, and familiar with pain"* (NIV). You see, even His Father rejected Jesus on the cross. Matthew 27:46 tells us, *"And about the ninth hour Jesus cried out with a loud voice, saying, 'Eli, Eli, lama sabachthani?' that is, 'My God, My God, why have You forsaken Me?'"* (ESV) God left Him alone because 2 Corinthians 5:21 says, *"For He made Him who knew no sin to be sin for us..."* (ESV). Jesus was alone to save us from Hell, and because of His choice to stay on the cross, rejected, we believers will be in the company of God forever. What a mighty God we serve.

4. Lastly, be intentional. As my brother taught me, as a disciple of Jesus Christ it's tough to be in a state of loneliness. If we are truly seeking biblical community and have the physical and mental capability, we should not remain lonely for a very long time.

Currently, at the time I am writing this book, I am single, meaning I'm currently not courting anyone. Guess what? I am okay with that. Why am I okay with that? Because I have developed friendships to help me live my life wholly devoted to Christ as I prepare myself for a spouse. Guys, we need people to help us walk through this life. My Facebook relationship status may or may not change when this book is finished; however, my hope is steadfast in the Lord.

Being *#CompletelySingle* is a great place to be as you will read and allow the Holy Spirit to speak to you through every flip of the page. You will read about some real-life stories of the struggle and how these principles are applied to my life. As I told a recent audience, I was raised in the church but I never heard this subject preached the way God has laid it out to me so plainly. I believe I had to go through it myself so I could show people that with God, nothing is impossible. Yielded to His Spirit, you also have access to supernatural strength.

This book was written from a male perspective, for males, because all humanity started with one person—a man. Now, I do believe and suggest that women read this book as well. This will help them to see what a biblically single man looks like before he asks to court or even marry. You can also give this book to teenagers so they can start learning what God's principles are for becoming wholly devoted to Him, and can begin living this lifestyle as well.

As I said, I do not believe that singleness is strictly a gift, but rather is a choice. I do provide you dating and courtship tips toward the back of the book. I gathered these from my personal life and my studies, from those around me who did it the right way, and from those who made mistakes and now provide boundary tips. However, the true gift is building a strong relationship with the Trinity while you are single, as you will discover in the pages ahead!

This book is jam-packed with information and godly principles. When they are applied, I believe they will change your life and the lives around you. So take some notes and leave remarks at the end of each chapter. Reflect on what's being said and how it is affecting your emotions and your soul. I'm excited to start this journey with you. For those like myself, who might have made mistakes in the past, my journey may seem to be impossible—and surprisingly, you are right. We each have our own stories and journeys in life. I can only walk my path, and you yours. You are wonderfully and uniquely made. You shouldn't strive to be anyone other than who God created you to be.

Andy Stanley said it best when he was talking to a

crowd of young singles here in Atlanta in 2011: "Become the person you are looking for is looking for." I personally believe that, biblically, you can become the person you are looking for. And we have provided principles in this book to help you become that person.

Now the next step is to turn the page and start a new journey. It will be tough, and you may experience some setbacks as I do sometimes; but if you put your full trust and hope in the Lord, I promise you will start seeing fruit from your labor.

This book is more than dating advice or relationship advice, which can be found on the Internet. These are biblical principles that, when applied, will help you in your quest to become a whole person before entering into your next relationship.

So I want to thank you for picking up this book. I am truly pumped about what the Lord is going to do in your life! Let's get started on the journey to becoming *#CompletelySingle*.

Part One:

Becoming the Right One

"Become the person you are looking for is looking for."

—Andy Stanley

Chapter 1
How to Die

And the Lord God formed man of the dust of the ground, and breathed into his nostrils the breath of life; and man became a living being.

— Genesis 2:7 (NKJV)

The Beginning

"Now, I'm just waiting on my rib," I exclaimed. This is how I ended my response on being obedient to God as a single. This statement was followed by gut-busting laughs from the audience. While I even chuckled a bit with the audience, I was very serious about what I was saying. Let me explain.

You see, I was invited to speak at a conference series called "Kingdom Relationships: Made In His Image," which three small-group leaders at my church, Victory World Church, put together. The topic for the night was how to be a godly man or woman. I was invited along with the praise and worship pastor from the young adult ministry, called Fusion, where I was the current prayer team leader.

Rebecca, the worship leader, had the floor first to give her answer on how to be obedient to God. However, after a few seconds, she turned to me and said, "I believe Damien has something to say about this." And so the baton was passed, and I didn't look back.

This whole scene was kind of surreal. Almost two weeks before the conference, God gave me a revelation at work that changed my life and made me realize this was the path He literally had placed me on for more than twenty years. I had simply asked God a question about relationships, and He had given me a profound response. Now fast forward to the conference, where I proclaimed before everyone, "What I am about to tell you will change your life, and I believe I need to write a book about it."

I know you will want to know what God showed me in Scripture about relationships and about how to become #CompletelySingle. So keep on reading!

Learning How to Die

When you look at this phrase, be honest: It's intimidating, isn't it? Who wants to die? I surely don't. Research studies have said that death is the second-most-feared thing behind public speaking. So why do we have to die to be completely single and wholly devoted to God?

"Because Adam, too, was dead—in the beginning." The first part of Genesis 2:7 reads, "*And the Lord God formed man of the dust of the ground...*" (NKJV). I think sometimes I read so quickly that I do not think about what is happening to different characters in the Bible. I personally had to mature in this area, learning how to slow down and allow the Holy Spirit to speak to me. When I slowed down, I started to see the multiple angles of a particular scripture, which is what happened with this study.

The Spirit asked me a simple question when I was studying this passage: "What was the state of man in the first half of this verse?" As I looked closely, I was shocked to see that man was already formed. My understanding of where the man was expanded because I slowed down. Why was this revelation so important? Because we see here that although he was formed, he had no life! He was known to be only flesh and bones. He was lifeless—or, we would say, he was dead.

The man did not have any recollection of who he was, what he was going to do, or what his purpose was. He also did not know who God was yet. You see, in this verse we see that the supreme eternal being—Jehovah (**Elohim**)—formed, framed, made, and molded man out of dust of the ground. However, man still did not have any sense of purpose. I believe this is a great place for us to start this journey to being #CompletelySingle.

We have to come to the realization and receive the revelation that, apart from God our Creator, we are nothing. No, really. Some scientists have found that we humans contain the same chemicals found in the ground. The total chemicals found in both the ground and human beings come to a whopping fifteen or sixteen components. That's it. And to purchase these chemicals in the 1980s would cost about $2.98.

In John 5:19, *"Jesus gave them this answer: 'Very truly I tell you, **the Son can do nothing by himself;** he can do **only** what he sees his Father doing, because whatever the Father does the Son also does.'"* He goes on in John 5:30 to say, *"**By myself I can do nothing;** I judge only as I hear, and my judgment is just, for I seek not to please myself but him who sent me."* (NIV)

If Jesus Himself recognized He was nothing and could do nothing without the Father, I believe this is a great place for us to begin as well. My friends, we can do nothing without God Himself giving us the ability to do so. If you want to start this healthy life devoted to God, a life of purpose and meaning like Christ's, you have to surrender your will, your plans, and your flesh to God.

To start this journey you have to recognize God alone as your Adonai! **Adonai** is an Old Testament Hebrew word meaning "Lord, Master, or Owner." I know these words are not popular in our society today. However, as we see in the life of Christ, He recognized that going lower actually elevated Him to His rightful place (Philippians 2:5–11). As followers of Christ, we must surrender as well in order to follow in His footsteps and advance His kingdom.

So How Do We Make Christ Our Lord?

The first thing we must do to make Jesus Christ our Lord is to become **completely** humble. This is done by confessing Him to be our Lord. Romans 10:9 says *"that if you confess with your mouth the Lord Jesus and believe in your heart that God has raised Him from the dead, you will be saved"* (NKJV).

I was blessed at an early age to accept Christ for myself. It actually happened after a traumatic event. When I was about seven or eight, I was playing kickball with my brothers and a couple neighborhood friends. One of the boys kicked the ball across the street, and I volunteered to go fetch it. After looking both ways, I jetted across the street like a star football wide-receiver. However, I must have not looked close enough because there was a car barreling down the road and then

BAM! The car hit me. Later I was told that the impact of the accident caused me to do a backward somersault. SPLAT! I hit the pavement hard.

I didn't know where I was, and I was a little dazed and confused. I could not feel my right foot, so I got up and hopped across the street to finish retrieving the ball. Yep, I had to "complete the task." This is a phrase my natural father continues to preach to this day. The driver and my brothers rushed to see if I was okay. And I was! No injuries at all.

God spared my life. That night when my dad came home, he asked me, "If you had died today, where would you have gone?" I told him, "I don't know." Well, he then proceeded to walk me through the prayer of salvation, and I was saved.

Now, it took a lot of work to figure out what that meant as I grew in my faith; I had to learn this throughout my life. However, that day I surrendered my life to God and told Him, "The most important relationship is with You!" This means all our mess needs to be given to God. The unforgiveness, bitterness, and ungodly soul-ties should be exposed and surrendered to God as well.

You see, I confessed, and I was saved. Also, Jesus gave me a gift: **the Holy Spirit!** This is a promise given not only to me but also to all man. God desires for not one of us to be lost or perish (2 Peter 3:9). We will be saved from death if we confess and surrender our lives to Christ. He has to become the captain of the ship and the Lord over our bodies. When we confess, we allow His Spirit, the same spirit that performed all His miracles and even raised Jesus from the dead, to live inside of us.

With God taking full control, we give up all our rights. We even have to let Him in as Lord over our finances, our professional lives, our goals, our relationships, and our health. Take some time and ask yourself, "Have I surrendered my all to God?" It doesn't matter if you are not saved or if you've been saved for thirty minutes or for thirty years—we **all** will have to humble ourselves and bow down to Christ one day. So what I am saying is this: What better day than today to surrender? Once we truly say "Yes!" to Him, He is then our Master—He becomes our Lord.

Secondly, we must do what He says. So many believers struggle with this one because they try to do this thing called life by themselves. They lean on their own understanding and then can't understand why they have so many problems and have not found their purpose in life yet. Shoot, I struggled with this one for a long time!

Solomon was the wisest man on earth, even though he didn't always follow this wisdom. Toward the end of his life, he started realizing some of his faults and jotted a lot of his thoughts down in the book of Ecclesiastes. Funny thing is, Solomon rarely practiced what he preached. This begs the question: Do we?

Now, in the book of Ecclesiastes we see a recurring theme throughout where everything is "meaningless," but toward the end we see Solomon came to his senses and provided an astounding revelation. Ecclesiastes 12:13 reads, *"Now all has been heard; here is the conclusion of the matter: fear God and keep his commandments, for this is the duty of all mankind"* (NIV).

Do we strive to keep His commandments? It's one thing to say, "I trust You God," but it goes to a whole new level when we say, "I will obey your commandments." I mean, if I look over my life and go back to those times when I was down or struggling in my walk with Christ, God shows me that my troubles appeared mostly because of my disobedience.

Now, don't get me wrong, I know that we live in a fallen world. We have an enemy, and people can be evil. Yet we can choose to follow His commandments any day of the week. That's our choice. This can sound burdensome to most of us since we tend to look through the same lens as the Pharisees did.

However, I really want you to get this revelation. God's laws given to Moses for the children of Israel were not meant to be just a list of commands. No, God's laws are good. They are not meant to harm us, but rather to help us stay in line. Jesus Himself said, *"Do not think that I have come to abolish the Law or the Prophets; I have not come to abolish them but to fulfill them."* He goes on to say that *"therefore anyone who sets aside one of the least of these commands and teaches others accordingly will be called least in the kingdom of heaven, but whoever practices and teaches these commands will be called great in the kingdom of heaven"* (Matthew 5:17, 19 NIV).

In the Old Testament there were 613 laws, also known as commandments. That is a lot. How can anyone follow all these laws on a daily basis? It would be extremely hard, and you would have to isolate yourself from people as well. Yet the Bible has an answer for us: Jesus said in John 14:15, *"If you love Me, keep My commandments"* (NIV). Our focus has to be on Jesus. We see in the following verse that when you do this, Jesus will pray that the Holy Spirit will help us.

We can't do this by ourselves, guys, even though so many of us try so hard. I had to learn this the tough way. Put your focus on Jesus and ask the Helper, the

Holy Spirit, if you should do this or that. When you feel that "check" or nudge in your spirit, you know it is the Holy Spirit talking to you. This has saved me from a lot of pain, and it will save you likewise. It's our choice to live moral lives, but the Holy Spirit is there to help as well.

Jesus offers this stark reality in Matthew 16: a true follower is someone who has given up his or her right to lead. Jesus has to become your Shepherd during this process—He has to become your Lord. As we journey together, discovering the next five principles of being completely single in God's kingdom, I believe we must keep Matthew 16:25 at the forefront of our minds: *"For whoever wants to save their life will lose it, but whoever loses their life for me will find it"* (NIV). Losing your life, as we just learned, means dying to self and surrendering your own will to Jesus Christ, as He did to His Father.

But the story doesn't stop there. Jesus brought a kingdom, and when we accept Him, our identity changes. We are no longer slaves or indentured servants; we are free. Galatians 5:1 tells us, *"It is for freedom that Christ has set us free. Stand firm, then, and do not let yourselves be burdened again by a yoke of slavery"* (NIV).

So, what then shall we be called? John 1:12 says we

shall be called *"sons of God"* (KJV). If the Holy Spirit is in us, we are now heirs to a greater kingdom in heaven and on earth. 1 Timothy 6:15 calls Christ the *"King of Kings and Lord of Lords"* (KJV). If Jesus Christ is our King, then we are now considered kings. If Jesus Christ is our Lord, then we are now considered lords.

What I am sharing is Good News and the message of a kingdom—a kingdom waiting for its sons and daughters to awake and claim what's rightfully theirs. When we are growing up, we learn how to serve because we are part of a family. However, our parents don't expect us to wear the chains of a slave while doing our chores. Why? Because we are their sons and daughters.

The enemy does not want you to gain this revelation. He wants you to stay with a slavery mindset and try to work your way to be accepted by the King. But I am here to tell you that you **are** a king. So walk in that revelation. We are the ones to learn first the culture of the kingdom of heaven, and then walk it out and reflect it here on earth. So what are we waiting for? Let's walk it out and rule!

Prayer for Surrender

Father, our prayer as we start this journey is this: "Not my will, but Yours be done." Give me the strength to surrender all to You, whether it's in my finances, my work, or my health. Father God, it's all Yours. God, I repent for all of my sins and for not putting You and Your kingdom first. Thank You for forgiving me. Show me the areas that are distracting me from giving myself completely to You and establishing Your kingdom on earth. I confess You as Lord of my life and I accept the gift of the Holy Spirit. Thank You for making me an heir to Your kingdom. It's in Jesus' name I pray. Amen.

Congratulations on surrendering your life to Christ. You are now born-again! We do encourage you to seek to show the world externally what just happen internally by being baptized by water. Please ask your local church for information on this process, taking the next step in your walk with Christ.

Reflection Section

Great perspective of
dying to ourselves to have
life with Christ in us.

"Too many people spend money they haven't earned, to buy things they don't want, to impress people that they don't like."

–Will Rogers

Chapter 2
How to Live

And the Lord God formed man of the dust of the ground, and breathed into his nostrils the breath of life; and man became a living soul.

— Genesis 2:7 (KJV)

"Power Nothing"

In 2014 I was sitting in the audience at our church here in Norcross, Georgia, called Victory World Church, and a guest speaker told a wonderful analogy. Toward the end of his message, he talked about the unique memory of most men—how they forget birthdays, anniversaries, and even their children's names. I don't have children yet, but I do forget names all the time. However, one thing a man will not forget is his first car. Yep ... he stated that his first car was a 1965 Oldsmobile F85. I am not a car person; however, I can concur and totally agree that we men are attached to our first car. My first car was a 1993 Toyota Camry, and her name was "Purple Urple." And I don't want to hear one peep out of you about her name, either!

Now, the speaker's first car was passed down from his father through his siblings to him. He stated that it had "power nothing." No power brakes, no power steering or power windows. All the car was useful for, was to get him from point A to B. "And when we get saved, we are only getting from A to B as well," he explained. However, the speaker went on to say that a couple years later, he bought another car that had "power everything." He would just sit in the car, pushing the button for the windows, watching them go up and down and just thinking about the workout he used to have rolling up the windows manually. The thing is, both of the cars could have transported him from A to B, but only one has power. He stated that God doesn't want us to go through this life toiling and working so hard, fighting against the flesh, when He promises in Act 1:8, *"But you will receive power when the Holy Spirit comes on you…"* (NIV). The question I want to ask you, which the speaker asked us that day, is this: "If God offers you an upgrade, why wouldn't you take it?"

Learning How to Live

What I have noticed as I have been blessed to live on this earth for more than thirty good, long years is that many Christians and followers of Jesus are awake, but they all seem to be walking zombies. They are not living an extraordinary life, which is the life God intended them all to live.

The second part of Genesis 2:7 says that God "*breathed into his nostrils the breath of life; and man became a living being*" (NKJV). When I looked up specific words in the original text in this small passage, three seemed to jump off the page. The word *breathed* is the word **naphach** in the Hebrew, and it means "to blow or to give up." *Breath* is the word **neshamah**; it means "spirit." Lastly, *life* or **chay** means "alive." If we put all of that together, we see Elohim gave up His Spirit into the nose of the man, which made the man come alive. Read that again!

Again, we see in the second part of this verse that after God gave up His spirit, man "*became a living being.*" The original Hebrew indicated this from the very moment man started to exist. Not only did the man (Adam) exist, he himself now knew it. He knew he was alive. He instantaneously received a soul, or a mind to think for himself and make his own choices. He could now choose to have a relationship with God the Father. This separates man from every other creature that was created, including angels and the animals. Man was made in the image and likeness of God Himself. Adam was created three-in-one, like the Trinity: He was formed physically. He was a spiritual being. He became psychologically advanced. All in the same moment!

One major thing we see here is that God did not create

His Spirit from the earth. He didn't use the elements of the earth to create a spirit to put inside man as He did with Adam's body from the dust. No, God had to extract what was already in Himself and give that up so we could live. Our God is awesome. He gave us a piece of Him. Human life could not have started unless man had received God's Spirit first. We must come to the understanding, or have a renewed revelation, that without His Spirit inside of us, we will not truly live—especially when it comes to our relationships.

My First Encounter with the Holy Spirit

I think this concept of living by the Spirit is widely misunderstood and misused. However, what I can share with you is my first interaction and encounter with the Spirit of God. After that you can make your own conclusion and ask God for a similar experience.

As a son of a pastor, I have seen the manifestation of the Baptism of the Holy Spirit in different arenas and churches around America. I have seen it affect people in different ways—people would laugh uncontrollably, cry, faint, run, dance, or roll on the floor. I've seen it all. However, I never experienced it for myself until I was in college while attending Bellarmine University in Louisville, Kentucky.

I was in grad school at the Rubel School of Business. I was struggling with my identity around this time, but I knew I needed a change. I had no real power, and I was trying to live a life of purity before God, but I kept on falling. Now, I promised my mother that I would not have sex before marriage; however, I still struggled with lust of the flesh and the eyes. I still struggled with watching things I should not watch, in order to please this stronghold keeping me down. I later found out it was the spirit of Belial that was the stronghold that had held me back from progressing in a life of total freedom in this way.

So one day in my room, I surrendered that lust over to God and asked God to fill me up with the Holy Spirit and baptize me. What happened next was amazing! I was literally brought to my knees and wept before God. Then I started to pray in a holy language, which we call "tongues" (Acts 10:46). I lost track of time, but it seemed as if I was down for more than an hour. It was incredible. Now, if I told you I forever stopped lusting and watching inappropriate things, which God hates, at that moment, I would be lying to you. However, I now had power to fight the urges—not by myself but, rather, with the help of the Spirit of God.

It was a long, grueling process to drive out the urges to succumb to the enemy's plans and thereby destroy everything God had planned for me. I am now learning how to be sensitive to the Spirit and how to turn away from things when the Spirit of God is being vexed in my life. Because of this, people around me can see the fruit of what God is doing in my life. And guess what? The people around me are becoming inspired and attracted—not only to what I am doing but also to God and what His kingdom has to offer.

Saved by the Nail!
A Story on Being Sensitive to the Spirit

One Wednesday night in early 2013 after Fusion, our young adult Bible study, I clearly heard a small voice inside my heart say, "Buy a tire." What? The voice continued to repeat, "Buy a tire." I purposefully drive without the radio, so I know I was undoubtedly hearing the voice of God. I soon remembered that I didn't have a spare in my trunk. This gave me the confirmation I needed to heed this voice. I didn't know why, but I felt it was very important to listen.

I immediately called the office and told my mother I would not be coming in on Thursday until I had bought a tire because God had told me to get one. I then phoned my mechanic and set up a time to get the tire the next day.

Thursday came, and we met at Pull-A-Part, a local junkyard, where I purchased a tire for about fifteen dollars. The next day was Friday, and I was preparing for my first game night to be introduced as the new prayer team leader because the current leader was being called to missions in South Korea. She was transitioning out, and I was coming in. However, I had to stop by the store to get items I had promised to bring for the party. I made the quick stop at the local Target. When I came back outside, guess what I saw and found? My tire was flat. Hallelujah!

This might be the wrong response to you, but not to me. You see, instead of complaining, I started to rejoice because God is so graciously faithful! He had warned me to buy a tire two days earlier, and I had listened to His voice. I praised God the whole time as I changed my tire in that parking lot. After I was done, I jumped in the car and phoned my mother with tears in my eyes, telling her about the miracle that just happened.

Let's think about this for a second. If God had not warned me, I probably would have missed the party. Or I could have been stranded on the highway. But there was also something about that nail. It was perfectly positioned to let the air out at just the right time to let me know I needed to change it. I could have been driving, and it could have popped, damaging my rim, which would have been costly. You see, I believe God saved me with a nail that day, as His Son did more than two thousand years ago on an old rugged cross.

The Bible says that God's sheep hear His voice; however, we must position ourselves to live by the Spirit so we can recognize who is speaking. There are several voices that speak to us, and we must determine whether it is the voice of the flesh, our own will or emotion, the voices of other people, the voice of the devil, or most importantly, the voice of God. Living in and by the Spirit will help us learn how to decipher what voice is leading—which leads us to our next section.

How Do We Live by the Spirit?

In Matthew 4:1–11 we see that before Jesus started His ministry, He fasted and prayed for forty days in the desert. However, verse one tells us that He was *"led by the Spirit."* Jesus recognized the voice of the Spirit! As we see in the story, Jesus also recognized the voice of the tempter, or the devil himself, too. We see that the devil tempted Jesus in three ways:

- **Lust of the Flesh:** *"If You are the Son of God, command that these stones become bread"* (Matthew 4:3 ESV).

- **Pride of Life:** At the top of the temple the devil said, *"If You are the Son of God, throw Yourself down"*

(Matthew 4:6 ESV).

- **Lust of the Eyes:** *"All these things I will give You if You will fall down and worship me"* (Matthew 4:9 ESV).

John told us in 1 John 2:16 that these three test will not go away. It reads, *"For everything in the world—the lust of the flesh, the lust of the eyes, and the pride of life—comes not from the Father but from the world"* (NKJV). As long as the adversary is loose, these temptations will always be readily available to fall into its trap. But how do we prepare ourselves appropriately and assertively, like Jesus resisting the schemes of the tempter, so we can live victorious lives for His kingdom?

Well, as you probably know from personal experience, it is a challenge not to fall into pleasing this flesh of ours, isn't it? Romans 8:13 says, *"For if you live according to the flesh, you will die; but if by the Spirit you put to death the misdeeds of the body, you will live"* (NKJV). There is life in living in the Spirit, and I can tell you by personal experience that it's encouraging when you know there is another person present to help you. As we learned in the introduction to this book, the Holy Spirit is our Helper, Counselor, and Comforter. He is here to help.

Also, I am going to make my disclaimer here: living by

the Spirit is not living by a long list of laws, regulations, or rules. I agree with Pastor Pete Briscoe, senior pastor of Bent Tree Bible Church in Carrollton, Texas, that it is more a "dance" than a following of marching orders. Please pray to the Holy Spirit to get this concept implanted deep in your soul before you continue reading this book! This is a very important revelation to receive, but more importantly to accept. It's a dance. However, while learning to live free and "dance" with the Holy Spirit, I've noticed a couple of lifestyle changes that match biblical principles and keep me following and flowing in the Spirit. You will receive some of these in this chapter and throughout the rest of the book as well.

Furthermore, I don't want you to think that there is always a 1–2–3 process to live by the Spirit. It is dangerous to get in the mindset of using the Holy Spirit for the gifts He has to offer (1 Corinthians 12), or even just His power. We already have a profession that allows you to buy time from a person and use them for their body. We should just mature to the place where we just want to spend quality time with Him, the Person.

So even though I will list some things that I recognize help me to stay in His presence, I really do not want you to look to them as ways to connect to a mystical being. My real desire, or you might even say my prayer for you, is that you earnestly seek to know the Holy Spirit and discover how wonderful He really is. Later in the book, we will see what a relationship with Him looks like.

But for now, let's dive in to seven life-altering lifestyle changes that will create a contagious radicalness! You may even recognize some of these changes from the story of Jesus in the desert in Matthew chapter 4. The following points are revelations given to me by God in my own life and walk that produce the fruit of living in the Spirit due to being baptized by Him. These seven principles will help propel you to live a completely single life before God.

A Life of Prayer

I was a prayer team leader for two years at my local church in the young adult ministry, Fusion. I must admit, I didn't know I even liked to pray. I used to despise talking in front of people, much less praying intimately to God the Father in front of others. However, as I was serving with the children's ministry at my church, I felt God prompting me to do something else. It was wild because I was praying to God one day and I really felt Him trying to lead me to serve in another area, but I didn't know where. I specifically heard "prayer team" one day, but I didn't know if that was God or myself speaking.

Then, one Wednesday night at church for a regular Fusion service, I sat down with a young man whom I had met one week earlier. Before I could really get into asking how his week was going, he said something shocking. "You know what?" he asked. "I'm thinking about joining the prayer team." I was like, "Wow! Okay, God, I know this is You." So I approached the leader, and within two-and-a-half months, the leader knew I was going to be the new leader. The rest is what they call history, my friends.

Maintaining or developing a life of prayer is essential for your spiritual growth and living by the Spirit. Did I know how to pray when I started? Not really, but I was willing to be molded by God. I hear a lot of leaders and lay members teach their followers and friends just to tell God what they feel when praying. For some reason, I just don't like this approach. I think it's just disrespectful to the Most High God to say what you want to Him. I see young people all the time do this to their parents, and they are soon punished for speaking any way they please. Ecclesiastes 5:2 puts it plainly: *Do not be rash with your mouth, and let not your heart utter anything hastily before God. For God is in heaven, and you on earth; therefore let your words be few"* (NKJV).

You must first understand that prayer is simply communicating with God. Yes, that means you must listen as well! If I can give you a quick guide to help you pray more effectively, I would use the acronym PRAY, which a lot of theologians use to teach this subject. I like it a lot because it sets a great foundation for you to start your prayer life off on the right foot.

P = Praise: We turn our eyes and thoughts from ourselves and honor God for who He is and what He has done. He is worthy to be praised!

R = Repentance: Confession and repentance should be a daily practice in our walk with Christ. It should be seen as an act of worship as we serve a Holy God who commands the same from His sons and His daughters.

A = Ask: James 4:2 tells us that *"you do not have because you do not ask"* (NKJV). However, we still have to ask God with the right motives. It starts with the heart. "God, search my heart and reveal to me what is not of You! Amen."

Y = Yield: Just as Jesus yielded to the Father's will, we are also called to surrender our lives totally to Him. Romans 12:1 says, *"Therefore, I urge you, brothers and sisters, in view of God's mercy, to offer your bodies as a living sacrifice, holy and pleasing to God—this is your true and proper worship"* (NIV).

A Life of Fasting

If you are like me, you like to eat! But as you will learn in
Matthew 4:4, *"man does not live on bread alone"* (NIV).
However, we see a society here in the United States
consumed by food, figuratively and literally.

I joke all the time that my brothers and I learned very
early to fast. Yes, we heard this from the pulpit from our
father, but we really didn't get the revelation at church.
Rather, we remember my father and mother fasting all
the time at home. I remember seeing my mother fast
more than I did my father. Now, that doesn't mean she
fasted more than him, or that it was a competition; I
am just saying I saw that she fasted in front of us more.
As kids, this was a great example to us, to see that we
could go without food and offer that time as sacrifice
to the Lord.

Also, we saw fasting at school. My brothers and I at-
tended a Catholic elementary school where they would
fast during Lent for forty days. Now, I must interject
something here. Some religions use fasting as a way
of just performing another act to please God. I must
caution against this way of thinking. When fasting to
perform an act toward God, it is no longer fasting but
starving yourself, and that does not do anything but
harm yourself, especially your health. Make sure your

heart is in the right place and that you prepare your body before you go on an extended fast for multiple days. (Also, consult a physician if you have any serious medical issues or are pregnant).

There are different types of fast you can go on. You can research these on any search engine; however, some of the most popular are the Daniel Fast, the liquid fast, or a complete fast in which you do not intake anything for a short period of time. Scriptures with which you should familiarize yourself before you fast would include Isaiah 58, Daniel 1:12–17, Daniel 10:2–3, Matthew 4:1–11, and Matthew 6:5–18.

Remember, we fast in secret. We don't post all over social media sites that we are fasting and say, "Woe is me, I'm so hungry!" or, "Look at what I am doing for King Jesus." I say to you, don't worry about praises from other people—God will openly reward you for His glory, not yours. That's a promise.

What are some benefits to fasting? There are several physical benefits, like resting your digestive system, lowering your blood pressure, and detoxing your body. Going on a fast can also increase your energy, cause you to rest properly, help eliminate allergies, increase concentration and focus, help with weight lost, and strengthen your immune system, which has led to physical and spiritual healings.

Also, fasting increases your spiritual sensitivity and disciplines you to listen to the Holy Spirit and His direction. Fasting creates a deeper hunger for the things of God and His Word, when you feed (study) on the word more than on food. Once we empty ourselves, we increase our capacity to take on more of the things of God. We receive answers to prayers, and His provision for us is loosened.

When we fast, we should pray for those who are bound, persecuted, and hungry. We pray to God to break the chains holding people back from seeing His freedom. We don't eat, but we pray that God will feed those people their daily bread of healing, salvation, and deliverance. We can also give away food that may rot in our refrigerators during times of fasting.

Finally, I suggest you limit your media intake. We have to remember that our eyes and ears are to be set apart as holy unto God. During a fast, especially, it is pertinent that you turn away from, and turn down, the noise and distractions in your life. You will learn how to hear the still, small voice of the Father. There are many voices vying for your attention, whether it's your flesh, conscience, will, or emotions, the enemy, or other people. Learning how to fast, along with prayer, helps you decipher the one true voice of the Holy Spirit, who will never lead you astray!

A Life of Praise and Worship

There was a song we used to sing at church all the time, "He Has Made Me Glad (I Will Enter His Gates)." It goes like this: "I will enter His gates with thanksgiving in my heart / I will enter His courts with praise / I will say this is the day that the Lord has made / I will rejoice for He has made me glad." This song was written by Leona von Brethorst from Psalm 100:4, which reads, *"Enter into His gates with thanksgiving, and into His courts with praise. Be thankful to Him, and bless His name"* (NKJV).

I cannot tell you how important it is to have a life of praise and worship. It's such a vital piece to a person's life and his or her success against the enemy. Let me define the two practices: Praise is expressing approval and admiration. Worship is the expression of adoring reverence or regard. We are called to praise God for what He has done for us as well as to worship God simply for who He is!

The body of Christ is sometimes anemic when it comes to the subject of praise and worship. Nevertheless, I do believe there is a generation who is starting to understand the importance of this subject. But it really is sad sometimes when you visit churches and think two or three songs will just take us into His presence. It literally is a tease sometimes because we are more worried about rushing to get to the message than staying in the presence. Below are three major things that I found can hinder your praise and worship. Read the questions and take a quick personal inventory of your life to see where you are.

Lust of the Flesh/Eyes

What stuff are you watching or doing to satisfy your flesh? Is it affecting your praise?

> *Let the Lord Jesus Christ be as near to you as the clothes you wear. Then you won't try to satisfy your selfish desires.* (Romans 13:14 CEV)

Pride

Are you a person who boasts a lot in front of your peers or feels the need to prove you right? Are you looking to make yourself famous instead of making Jesus famous? Is pride affecting your worship?

> *Pride* [a haughty, arrogant spirit] *goes before destruction....* (Proverbs 16:18 NKJV)

> *In your relationships with one another, have the same mindset as Christ Jesus: Who, being in very nature God, did not consider equality with God something to be used to his own advantage;*

rather, he made himself nothing by taking the very nature of a servant, being made in human likeness. And being found in appearance as a man, he humbled himself by becoming obedient to death—even death on a cross! (Philippians 2:5–8 NIV)

Entitlement

Do you feel entitled, as if someone or some organization owes you something? Are you offended at someone, or do think you deserve an apology? Are you harboring bitterness or unforgiveness? Yet the only reward we truly deserve is death when we really stop to think about it.

> *For the wages of sin is death, but the gift of God is eternal life in Christ Jesus our Lord.* (Romans 6:23 NIV)

> *Therefore if you bring your gift to the altar, and there remember that your brother has something against you, leave your gift there before the altar, and go your way. First be reconciled to your brother, and then come and offer your gift.* (Matthew 5:23–24 NKJV)

> *And be kind to one another, tenderhearted, forgiving one another, even as God in Christ forgave you.* (Ephesians 4:32 NKJV)

A Life of Hatred

I know this section is throwing you off a little. I did this on purpose. Our God is a God of love (1 John 4:8). However, God cannot stand it when we sin. As a matter of fact, He hates sin, and Proverbs 6:16–19 gives us several sins He truly hates. Furthermore, we must decide to hate them as well. I think we sometimes fall into a religious life of grace, which is very important and biblical, but have we truly made a heart change to hate the sin that easily entangles us? Now, this does not mean we should start hating people. The Bible says to love your neighbors as yourself, and we are commanded to pray for our enemies. Nonetheless, we must hate the sin.

We have to develop this hatred of sin so that when we sin, which we all do at times, it's like a horrible taste in our mouths. For example, if your co-workers are trying to involve you in a gossip session, it can be very tough to avoid. I personally still struggle at times not to get caught in the middle of such gossip. However, we must learn to hate this sin and walk away.

When you do sin and repent, the Bible clearly says in Romans 8, there is no condemnation for those who are in Christ, and we should not feel guilty or shameful because we are made new. We have to keep on pursuing this life of sanctification—of spiritual cleansing. One way to do this is to pray to God and say, "Father, teach us how to love what You love and hate what You hate. Amen." This is a very strong prayer we can pray starting today!

A Life of Reading and Studying the Word of God

Reading the Word of God is a pivotal piece of living in and by the Spirit. God speaks through His word! The Bible tells us in Hebrews 4:12a, *"For the word of God is living and powerful, and sharper than any two-edged sword..."* (NKJV). It lives and has the power to speak to any and every situation you are going through. However, I am encouraging you not just to read God's Word, but to study it as well. Do you remember in Matthew 4 when the devil knew the word as well as Jesus did? Therefore, reading it is a great start, but studying and then applying it is where you gain the power.

My life verse, which is also my favorite verse, is Joshua 1:8: *"This Book of the Law shall not depart from your mouth, but you shall meditate in it day and night, that you may observe to do according to all that is written in it. For then you will make your way prosperous, and then you will have good success"* (NKJV). I know everyone wants to be successful in some capacity, and the Bible is very clear here how to begin and start your success.

So how do we study the word of God? Well, I get this question a lot, and I am going to give you a couple things I do to help me study God's word. Now, there are additional things you can do, but here I want to give you a foundation to start receiving life-altering revelation on a consistent basis. Meditating on what you have studied will develop success as well. You will then be more apt to apply the biblical principles to everyday life situations you will encounter.

Tips on Studying the Word of God:

1. Become a child. Matthew 18:3–4 says, *"Assuredly, I say to you, unless you are converted and become as little children, you will by no means enter the kingdom of heaven. Therefore whoever humbles himself as this little child is the greatest in the kingdom of heaven"* (NJKV). Remember to take on the manner of a child when you start studying the Bible as well. Be open and teachable, and ask a ton of questions. You might have received a revelation from God one time; however, as you continue to study His word, there will be deeper revelations that only a child can see.

2. Pray to the Holy Spirit before you open your Bible. Ask the Holy Spirit to reveal something new to you since He knows **all** (1 Corinthians 2:10–11).

You can also ask spiritual leaders for insight on passages or share newfound revelations with them. I am tremendously blessed to have a father who is a pastor and theologian, to whom I can reach out. Develop relationships at your local church and, again, ask a lot of questions.

3. I suggest not using your cell phone to study the Bible. You might have too many distractions, like text messages, phone calls, or other updates. An electronic tablet could work. I recommend these translations: KJV, NKJV, ASV, ESV, NIV, and the NLT. I personally do not recommend using the MSG version to study the Bible.

4. Things to look for while you are reading include names, places, things, repetition, numbers, ages, years, months, times of day, events, holidays, particular statements that stand out, and the context of the passage. Other elements that can be examined are quotations, similes, metaphors, allegories, and parables.

    There is also the term in theologian circles called "the law of first mention." This is where a word shows up for the first time and there is significance for that word placement. There are similar "laws" for scriptures that speak of different events simultaneously (law of double reference) and multiple scriptures that describe the same event in different ways (law of recurrence).

Here are some examples of questions you can ask: "Why was Jesus in the Jordan River? What does Jordan mean in this particular passage? Was there a similar event in the Old Testament—a type or a shadow—to which I can compare this event?"

5. Purchase a *Strong's Exhaustive Concordance,* or find it online. This book defines the Hebrew and Greek of each word in the Bible, typically the KJV translation. Some concordances will also give you all of Jesus' miracles, parables, and prayers. Usually a Strong's Concordance will provide historical data with the lineage of Christ as well. I have also seen the Thayer's Greek–English Lexicon used as a study tool.

6. Commentaries: For a New Testament Commentary, I would recommend author William Barclay. For an Old Testament Commentary, check out the *Holman Old Testament Commentary.* Finally, for a five-book collection that covers Genesis through Revelation, try Thru the Bible by J. Vernon Mc-Gee. He is very adept at explaining the Mosaic laws behind certain events. You will probably need

a *Strong's Concordance* to find out the definitions of certain key words.

A Life of Connection to Others

Hebrews 10:24–25 says, *"And let us consider one another in order to stir up love and good works, not forsaking the assembling of ourselves together, as is the manner of some, but exhorting one another..."* (NKJV). In the introduction of this book, we really hammered this point home, but it is important to return to it. I am in fact preaching to myself when I say we need each other. To forsake means to abandon, renounce, or give up. We should not abandon meeting together, because we need each other to push forward the kingdom of God.

To be real with you, I personally have tendencies to isolate myself. I like being alone because I can think, read a good book, or just sleep. However, sometimes I can find myself staying in my room for a couple days at a time. That is not healthy, so I decided that I have to be more intentional about meeting with other people, even though that is not my nature. You may relate to this as well. You may be an introvert who likes playing video games and surfing the Internet or social media, and you wonder why you are lonely. Be intentional, my friend. Join a youth group, volunteer with a young adult ministry, or participate in a club for believers, like

Fellowship of Christian Athletics if you are an athlete. Even though this may take a lot out of you, it is so worth it!

One thing I did was pray for accountability. Not only did God provide me with some great individuals for this purpose, but in the process they became lifelong friends. Some also became prayer partners: we pray together at least once a week and confess our sins to one another so we can be, and remain, healed (James 5:16).

A Life of Taking Risk

The Bible is clear that without faith, it is impossible to please the Lord (Hebrews 11:6). Believe me, using your faith is taking a big risk. I can only speak from personal experience; however, I had to learn that this is probably one of the most important points in truly living.

As the prayer team leader, I wanted to please people and make sure I put on a façade that I was living a perfect life. But to be honest with you, that life stunk, and I could not really be myself and become the man God created me to be. Therefore, I started to place others' opinions in godly perspective. I am not here to please people but, rather, the Lord.

Now, not living to please others is a risky lifestyle, and it didn't start with my leadership of the prayer team.

No, it started earlier. It started when I acted in my first play, and when I competed in the dance contest in middle school and won. My risk-taking continued when I went and tried out for baseball and basketball even though I had never played before. However, it really bloomed when I started to write my first book in 2007.

You see, I had received this great idea from my mother to write a book to help people, just like you and me, achieve their dreams in life. Called *How to Load Your Truck*, it was based off some lessons I had learned from working at UPS. Yet just a few months earlier, before I sat down at my computer to write that book, one of my teachers told me my writing was not up to par for a graduate-school level. At this point, I was still trying to finish up my MBA. If I didn't really know how to write a paper, how in the world could I write a book?

But guess what—I didn't care. I felt the Lord was leading me to do it, so I took the risk. After I finished the manuscript, I asked my lawyer what he thought. He really didn't know if the UPS law office in Cincinnati would accept my manuscript because within the book I included UPS "keys" for loading a package car, as well as Bible references. He suggested I remove them, yet I did not. Why? Because I had followed the Lord's leading in including the keys and biblical references, so others' opinions on those matters were ultimately of no consequence. A couple of weeks later, they approved my book! Now, I have completed five books, and four have been published. I'm writing this one now, too, which is also a risk.

So you see my point. From trying out for sports teams to writing books to starting a business to sharing my faith, and even going on job interviews, I maintained an attitude of risk-taking, which I then applied to the prayer team. Now, I did not intentionally go around the church trying to hurt people's feelings or be rude, offensive, and disrespectful. That would have been foolish and prideful. Rather, I really wanted to see what the early church leaders experienced in sharing the faith, and to see "sun stand still" prayers answered. Joshua 10:12 tells us the story of how God supernaturally answered the prayers of Joshua to stop the sun from setting, and I wanted to start praying big prayers just like Joshua. I wanted to believe that I could communicate with God and then see the things I prayed for actually come into being.

Do you know what started to take place? We saw miracles. In fact, there were so many that I'm seriously contemplating writing a book on those events that happened—and will continue to happen.

One thing that really changed my whole life and helped

me with this new outlook was how I viewed reading the Bible. This is key in walking our life in the Spirit: I took a major risk and decided to **believe** first, before I opened the word of God and started to read it. How could I do this? How could I believe first, before ever reading or re-reading a passage? Because I developed a relationship with God that let me know what He says is true.

Oftentimes we read books to determine if we can believe or learn the material, no matter what we are reading. However, with the Bible, we should believe first and then read, which helps us strengthen our faith in the God we serve. We can afterward take that same faith and accomplish the same types of things Jesus and His disciples did on the earth. Not only that, but we are also called to do greater things than the early church leaders did (John 14:12)!

One thing I am learning is that I don't have to know all the ABCs of praying for someone or asking for healing for someone from God. What I mean is, we can waste time or deny people an encounter with God because we feel inadequate or don't know exactly what Jesus said before He prayed for people to be healed. The Bible, on the other hand, encourages us simply to pray without ceasing. When I started risking my faith in believing first, I began seeing more supernatural miracles with my natural and spiritual eyes!

Finally, the Bible states in 1 Peter 4:6, *"For this reason the gospel was preached also to those who are dead, that they might be judged according to men in the flesh, **but live according to God in the spirit**"* (NKJV). One of the major reasons I am writing this book is that in my short time on this earth, I have experienced what it means to live by the Spirit. And yes, I have failed many times in my personal life, and I have been wrong a lot. However, I serve a God who forgives. It is a big risk to live radically and to be called crazy for your stance on living for God and by the Spirit. People don't believe me sometimes about what I have seen; however, there are others who have been there and are hungry on how to live this way even more fully. The best advice I have for you is to surrender and trust God with your life, and He will mold you.

So how do you know you are finally living by the Spirit of God? Is there proof or evidence that the Spirit is in me and on me? My answer is in Galatians 5:22–23, which says, *"But the fruit of the Spirit is love, joy, peace, longsuffering, kindness, goodness, faithfulness, gentleness, self-control. Against such there is no law"* (NKJV). When you start seeing these characteristics manifested in your life, you know that God is entrusting you to advance His kingdom. But it's your decision when you are going to surrender your life to receive the power of the Holy Spirit. The choice is yours!

Now, if you are ready to receive the power of the Holy Spirit and be baptized by the third Person in the Trinity of God, pray this prayer with me…

Prayer for Life

Heavenly Father, at this moment I come to You. I thank You that Jesus saved me. I pray that the Holy Spirit might come upon me. Lord Jesus, baptize me now in the Holy Spirit. I receive the baptism in the Holy Spirit right now by faith in Your Word. May the anointing, the glory, and the power of God come upon me, and into my life right now. May I be empowered for service from this day forward. Thank You, Lord Jesus, for baptizing me in Your Holy Spirit. Amen.

Reflection Section

_____

_____

_____

_____

_____

_____

_____

_____

_____

_____

_____

_____

_____

Love bears all things, believes all things, hopes all things, endures all things. Love never fails.

—1 Corinthians 13:7

Chapter 3
How to Be a Good Steward

Then the Lord God took the man and put him in the Garden of Eden to tend and keep it.

— Genesis 2:15 (NKJV)

My First Job

Do you know what a PK is? Yep, a Preacher's Kid. You know, preachers' kids get a bad rap. I mean, we are put on this platform where we are expected not to make any mistakes at church, but we are expected to be the worst of all children at the same time. It's a weird oxymoron. Although I haven't asked my two brothers this, however, I personally would not change it for the world. I have seen firsthand what ministry can do to a family and the sacrifices that go into serving God, not only on a weekly basis but also daily. I have traveled and seen diverse churches all over this nation while some believers have only seen the "us four and no more" churches in their proverbial city they call home. It really is a treat.

Another major treat was to be introduced to the true

God of the Bible at an early age and to learn His commandments and unending wisdom. However, I must confess to you that even though I had access to this great wisdom, I really didn't steward it properly as far as living it out. I was more devoted to being popular in sports, especially in my high school days. My ears started to tingle when clergymen from the pulpit or classrooms would recite well-known verses about finding a mate or getting a girl. I would especially try to memorize those! Having a girl and sports was the thing— my dream. One verse that was quoted often on finding a female was Proverbs 18:22, which states, *"He who finds a wife finds a good thing, and obtains favor from the Lord"* (NKJV). Shoot, I wanted to read the Bible then!

So that's what I did. I heard the words of the preachers and wanted to follow the Bible. I searched for and found my first girlfriend in high school. Yippee! However, this relationship ended horribly within a matter of months. Several things contributed to the break-up. For instance, one time I spent a whole twenty-four hours on the phone with this girl. This is a big no-no when courting, or in my case at the time, dating. We will talk about some helpful biblical principles for courting in our last chapter of this book.

Another significant factor that ended our relationship was my transportation. You see, I lacked the funds to own a car. This prohibited us from going out on dates together without being chaperoned by family members or, even worse, our parents. So she broke up with me.

Man, I was hurt! A good guy who tried to do right but was dumped for not having a vehicle. So what did I do? I no longer cared about sports that much. I wanted to prove that I was a man now, so I got my first real job. Where did I work? A family-owned mortgage company and hair salon called All-in-One. And no, I did not "do" women's hair. Nope, I swept and mopped it up, though. I was proud of myself. I was finally working and making my own money!

Work in itself was created to be a good thing, and there are several benefits to working, as we will see in this chapter. Even though I stepped into my first job because of a horrible break-up, it was good for me to start learning how to live a self-disciplined life and have responsibilities, in order to learn how to steward.

Was I now ready to find a wife and get married? Not exactly. Throughout this book you will continue to see God's hand in and on my life. I believe I am currently in the place He wants me to be.

Learning How to Be a Good Steward

In Genesis 2:15 we see that the Lord God *took* the man and placed him in the Garden of Eden. Let's unpack this a little further together.

God *took* the man. Researching the Hebrew word for took, we find that this verse says God carried away, brought, placed, established or rested the man in the Garden. The Garden in this particular text can be defined as a fence or hedge, for protection or defense. Here, God created a place that was His very presence, where man could be protected. God placed Adam, the first man, in the Garden, and He instructed Adam to start working. You see, as the man worked in the presence of God, there was safety. This begs the question: What happens to this "hedge of protection" when we step out of His presence?

Now, Eden was no ordinary place. When researching the word Eden, we find a wonderful definition. In fact, several meanings show up in the Hebrew: "delightful," "presence," "house of pleasure," "(open) door," and "begin to build." So we see that this place, which scholars cannot find, was much more than a geographic place; it was actually the presence of God. It was a presence that was very delightful and pleasing to dwell in, where there was a door to come and go as Adam pleased, back and forth from heaven. Not only that, but Adam was also able to start building there—this was the area where he started to work. You see, God's desire was ultimately to abide and work with man in His presence for eternity.

Which brings us to this question: Why did God place the man in the garden? God created the place so Adam could work and be a good steward of what God had originally created. A steward is simply a manager, and Adam was now put in place to learn how to manage, to govern, and more specifically, to have dominion over the land (Genesis 1:28). God is King in heaven. His original plan was to colonize the earth with the same kingdom principles that are in heaven. This is why the word dominion was used. Dominion is a kingdom term, which means to have "sovereign rule."

Toward the end of Genesis 2:15, we see that Moses, the writer of Genesis, was inspired to describe the man's purpose in the Garden as working, tending, cultivating, and keeping it:

> *Then the Lord God took the man and put him in the Garden of Eden to tend [work, cultivate] and keep it.* (NKJV)

I really like the verb *cultivate* here, which expresses

three meanings that jump out in my spirit. To cultivate originally meant to prepare and work land in order to raise crops. Secondly, *cultivate* can mean "to develop or improve by education or training; train; refine" (dictionary.com). Lastly, to cultivate can mean to promote or foster something through relationship—such as friendship or love. You see, cultivation was not only supposed to be used for working the land; we will see that you can also apply the concept of cultivation to your future spouse.

The word *keep* also shows us a lot about God's intent for us working in His presence. This word, when defined in the original text, means to guard, to protect, to beware, to wait, and to watch. Adam not only had the job to cultivate and prepare the land, but he also had to protect it from the enemy. He had to beware of the danger that may lurk and try to steal the very presence that God had given Him.

Therefore, Adam had a handful of responsibilities to worry about in the presence of the King. Ultimately, however, He was called to steward the presence of God, and this was one huge responsibility. But as we found, it was delightful; it was a pleasurable place, and God had set Him up for success!

So Where Are You?

Did you answer the question yet? This can be a question for both men and women, but I intend it especially for men. The late Myles Munroe said it best when he remarked that God first created the place, then put the thing there to make it successful. For example, God created the water for the sea creatures, and if we take these animals out of the water, they will die. The same is true for plant life. He created the ground first and put plants there to be successful. If you remove the plants, what happens over time? They will wither up and die. Finally, God created Eden as an open door to the presence of God so we could be successful. However, because of the fall of man, we were taken out of the presence of God.

The 1990s film Total Recall comes to mind when thinking about man being removed from the presence of God. Toward the end of the film, Douglas Quaid, played by Arnold Schwarzenegger, landed outside the safe, controlled zone where the air was clean and entered into contaminated air, causing him to suffocate and almost die. This is the same thing that happens with us when we stand outside His presence: we malfunction every time! We also become dysfunctional, thereby bringing harm and even death to each other because we have not found our way back to God's presence.

But guess what? Jesus is the key! Jesus is the way back to the presence of God (John 14:6).

So again I ask you: Where are you? Are you in His presence? As men, we need to learn how to enter back into the presence of God so we can be successful. Women, if you find a man working, that is a very good thing; however, the first place you need to find your man is in the presence of God.

You must also beware of the enemy's schemes here. He has set up places where there might be a **false presence**. Some clubs and bars with lewd and obscene music may create a false presence, where you are then under the influence of the enemy, which leaves your judgment inhibited. Both women and men need to be very careful here. Is a man in the presence of God—or better yet, does he know how to get there? How does this man steward the presence of God first and foremost? Does he go to church? Does he read and study the Word of God? Is He unashamed to worship God in spirit and in truth? Trust me, you will know He has been in the presence of God because there will be visible fruit radiating out of his life.

Men, this is our challenge. We have to get back to the presence of God! We have a great opportunity here. As we enter and stay in the presence of God, we can learn how to cultivate and keep the very women God will send our way. Cultivating your wife is learning how to train her in something new— fostering her, preparing her for the world, educating her in business (if she doesn't know already), promoting her dreams and vision, refining (cleansing) her with the word, and having her work on something together with you. These are the things that will get a woman excited and stay excited to be with you.

Finally, keeping your future wife is simply guarding her heart and watching out for her. You see, God teaches you how to protect your garden while you are at work so you can learn how to protect her garden at home after you are married. And the church said, "Amen!"

Are You a Good Steward of God's Provision?

One thing I want to drive home in this chapter is that we are Kings. However, we are also stewards of our heavenly King's possessions, property, and glory. Psalm 24:1–2 puts it plainly: *"The earth is the Lord's, and all its fullness, the world and those who dwell therein. For He has founded it upon the seas, and established it upon the waters"* (ESV). We are His, and everything we own is His as well. With that said, I will submit to you that what we do with what we have is more important to the King than how much we have. How we work and steward what we have is of great importance to God.

Work is essentially worship. As I stated earlier, it is good. While working we are thanking God for giving us the ability to work, and we will offer this time of stewardship as a sacrifice to God. One of the best examples of this in the Bible is Samuel, in the book of 1 Samuel, chapters 2 and 3, when Samuel was working in the Temple under Eli. As I was studying this Scripture passage, I was shocked to see how Samuel himself heard the voice of God by working well. The following passage is from a *Thoughts From The Box* devotional series I did on positioning oneself to hear God's voice:

> We cannot go into our prayer time with a know-it-all attitude; we must humble ourselves to the one who knows all. Remember, God is omniscient!

> [Another] thing that stuck out to me during my study time can be found in 1 Samuel 2:18, which says: *"But Samuel was ministering before the Lord—a boy wearing a linen ephod [embroidered vestment]"* (KJV). This is the second time we see Samuel ministering before the Lord. However, in the Hebrew this word is translated as "worship."

As we learn how to position ourselves, we must also determine how to worship God—not just any type of worship, but a holy and set-apart type of worship. Jesus tells the Samaritan woman, in John 4:24, that a time has come when true worshipers will worship *"in spirit and truth"* (NKJV). We can see evidence of this even in the way Samuel dressed. Samuel wore the ephod, which literally was a garment that God directed priests to create and wear to show they were set apart (Exodus 28).

[Yet another] way that Samuel teaches us about positioning ourselves is found in 1 Samuel 3:1: *"Samuel was ministering before the Lord under Eli"* (ESV). This is the third time we see Samuel ministering—and, as we now know, worshiping—but in this context the worship is slightly different. As we read on, the passage says, *"In those days the Word of the Lord was rare; there were not many visions."* In the original Hebrew text, ministering also means "waiting."

As I was meditating on this, the Spirit of God said, "Add a K to your worship." You see, as Samuel was waiting on the Word of God, you would find him Wor'K'-shiping under Eli. As we wait on God's divine word, we must be found working, just as Elijah found Elisha working in the field before he went into the ministry.

We should also honor God with the work we perform with our hands, which can be seen as a form of worship as well. Colossians 3:23–24 says, *"Whatever you do, work at it with all your heart, as working for the Lord, not for human masters, since you know that you will receive an inheritance from the Lord as a reward. It is the Lord Christ you are serving"* (NIV).

Samuel was set apart because his work was set apart.

There are four things I have learned to help me focus on God, rather than on myself, when it comes to stewarding God's possession and His provision while I work. Yes, God is my Jehovah Jireh—"The Lord Will Provide." However, He gives us work to help provide for ourselves and build self-discipline as we grow into His ultimate purpose for our lives. It also gives me a different perspective when I work not unto man, but unto God. As you work, please remember four principles from author E. Jay O'Keefe, which I list and expound upon below:

1. All provision has duration on the earth. In Ecclesiastes 3 we see that there is *"a time and a season"* for all things. Two of those things are birth and death. For certain, each of us has an expiration date. Therefore, the things we have or are working on currently will have to be transferred to someone else, whether it's our family members or the state, if there is no will. One thing is for certain: it's going somewhere. This perspective makes me think about working not for carnal things, which can bring a little pleasure, but on things of eternal value. I believe this is the purpose of our work. Don't work only for the dot, but also for the whole line.

2. All provision has a purpose and responsibility. When I work now, I try to see the purpose of what I am doing. As a result, I want to do everything with excellence—not to perfection, because that is not attainable, but with some sense of pride that God gave me this work to do on this earth.

One thing I have to work on is being cognizant of the possessions I have, such as my home and car. Sometimes, because of busyness, I tend to not appreciate what God has given me, and I therefore lack the sensibility to keep these things in order, like cleaning my room. We have to be aware that all we have is a gift from God, even our time and our money. We have to be able to use and sacrifice these things for the advancement of the kingdom of God. For me, that means spending time with the less fortunate. Offering your house to those who need a place to stay and giving your tithe and offering to your local church are also examples. Finally, we should seek to pay back our debts, pay our bills, save, and invest. We have a responsibility to be good stewards of the provisions placed in our hands because they all have a purpose attached to them.

3. Stewardship of provision is rewarded. We have to keep in mind that God is so gracious **all** the time, He allows us to be rewarded for stewarding His provision well. In the Old Testament we saw this to be a promise (Deuteronomy 28:1–14). However, in the New Testament we are promised Christ. We have to come to the realization that in Him we have all that we need.

Now, Jesus Christ does speak on stewarding our talents and being faithful with the little, that we might one day earn the opportunity to steward more. However, that's not a precursor for obtaining things or possessions. Jesus was preparing our hearts so that if God were gracious to give us things, we would know how to act or steward accordingly. Jesus is the biggest reward in the new covenant. I love how David Platt, the author of the New York Times' bestseller Radical, said it at the D6 Conference in 2011: "Jesus is not a means to an end, He is the end."

4. Poor stewardship of provision brings penalties. Now, a stark reality is this: if we don't steward well, we are prone to lose what God has entrusted in our hands. Proverbs 13:22b says that *the wealth of the sin-*

ner is stored up for the righteous" (NIV). We see this all the time, don't we? People lose cars and homes sometimes because they don't steward their money correctly, or they overspend in areas in which they should have been more careful.

Budgeting our time and finances helps us live a life of purpose and responsibility. Yes, we may fall on hard times; however, we must do all we can to soften the fall on most occasions. Job was an upstanding man, and he gave us some wise words to help us change our perspective on who is really in control. As Job 1:21 says, *"Naked I came from my mother's womb, and naked shall I return there. The Lord gave, and the Lord has taken away; blessed be the name of the Lord"* (NKJV).

Prayer of Stewardship

Father, help me be a good steward of what You place in my hands, especially our relationships and, most importantly, Your presence. If I become complacent in any area in my life, please shine a light on it! Help me to remember that whatever I do, whether I eat or drink, I am doing it for Your glory and You alone. In Jesus' name I pray. Amen.

Reflection Section

_____

_____

_____

_____

_____

_____

_____

_____

_____

_____

_____

_____

Let love be without hypocrisy. Abhor what is evil. Cling to what is good. Be kindly affectionate to one another with brotherly love, in honor giving preference to one another…

—Romans 12:9–10 (NKJV)

Chapter 4
How to Stay Within Boundaries ...
and Out of Bondage

And the Lord God commanded the man, saying, "Of every tree of the garden you may freely eat; but of the tree of the knowledge of good and evil you shall not eat, for in the day that you eat of it you shall surely die."

— Genesis 2:16–17 (NKJV)

The Hotel Room

The following account is a true story and a great example of why we all need boundaries. I will give you the details from my perspective and try to be as honest as possible while still keeping this PG-13. I believe we have to be authentic if we really desire to seek the healing we so desperately want and need in our lives. So sit back, relax, and grab some popcorn.

One day while preparing financials for a pastor friend of mine, I received a text message from a young lady I was trying to **stop** talking to. The struggle was real. Now, first of all, I knew I should have stopped talking to this young lady because our belief systems did not line up at all. I believe in the Trinity and that Jesus

Christ is the only way to restore our relationship with the Father (John 14:6). Meanwhile, she believed (or may still believe, I have no idea) in Hinduism and was studying divination and palm reading. Do you see the conflict? I know you are shaking your head at me!

Well, the biblical term here is being "equally yoked," and we were nowhere close to that. If you are not familiar with this term, it is derived from the farming industry, when the farmer would place a wooden crosspiece over the neck of two animals, such as oxen. This crosspiece would be connected to a plow, which would help till the ground—so long as the yoked animals were similar and moved in the same direction. Likewise, in relationships, it is smart to court a person who has the same beliefs as you, or else you will be pulling each other in opposite directions, causing unnecessary stress to the relationship. Got it?

Okay, back to the story. Well, this young lady worked for the airline industry and was telling me that she was coming into town later that evening. For some dumb reason, and I mean dumb, I responded that I would like to see her. The truly crazy part is that she said, "Damien you are going against your boundaries. But okay." She agreed to see me. I reassured her we could just hang downstairs or something. Yeah, right!

So around 1 a.m., I got the call and I headed out to the hotel. When I reached the hotel, the valet took my keys and I headed to her room. I arrived at her room and was greeted with a hug.

However, I didn't feel right even being in that room. I knew I was testing waters that were too hot and was trying to see how close I could get without sinning. Raise your hand if you know what I mean?

So we started playing silly games and verbally sharing what we felt about each other at that moment. I was getting nervous because this situation was getting out of control. I decided to leave, but she asked me for one last hug—and BAM! That was it. We embraced for a long time, and I was caught in a web of overwhelming feelings. I then started to kiss her neck, and we fell onto her bed. She asked me, "Do you really want to do this?" I didn't even answer her question.

But then something miraculous happened: the temperature in the room skyrocketed. Now, yes, I was hot because my hormones were jumping up and down like those of a kid who is wide open for a lay-up on the basketball court. Yet I am telling you, the room temperature went to Hades. I asked the young lady, "Why is it so hot?" In reply she kissed my neck, which was the craziest thing I had ever experienced.

Then I tried to continue with the kisses below her neck, but at that point I clearly heard the Spirit of God say, **"This is not your wife."** Boom! I was done.

I told the young lady, "I have to go." She wanted one more hug at the door, and she didn't want to let me go. However, I pushed her off of me a little and jetted out the door. Then, when I got to my car, I did something really low to top off the night: I told the valet on duty that night to put the charge on the young lady's room. I was so immature, right? I knew it was the end of that relationship.

I quickly texted my accountability partner, and he called early that morning to discipline me. I actually apologized to the young lady a couple days later for leading her on. What I did was wrong, and I had placed myself in a hypocritical situation. God even showed me that He had given me ways to get out of that situation earlier, but I had wanted to test whether I was strong enough. It's only by the grace of God that I got out of that room without going all the way—and perhaps even getting her pregnant because we didn't have condoms. Stupid! And this, my friends, is why we all need boundaries.

Learning How to Stay Within Boundaries

In Genesis 2:16–17, we see the author quotes God as He is giving Adam the first laws in His new kingdom. One thing we must understand from this story is that God's original intent was to take the same culture and kingdom of heaven and have it on earth. We must ask God to help us reprogram our biblical studies accordingly and apply kingdom principles in studying the word of God.

The first line of Genesis 2:16 shows us one of the major principles that is understated in our Western theology: it says that *"the Lord God **commanded** the man."* There are two principles of a kingdom that resonate right here. First, a king's word is law. What does this mean? It means our God, the King, is absolute; the words from His mouth are absolute and final law.

Secondly, a king's decree is unchanging. You see, in our American democracy, laws change due to the public's popular opinion or vote! In other governments the leader may choose to change the laws if he or she feels it's a good idea. You will usually see that style of governing in a dictatorship. But once the king issues a decree, by contrast, it cannot be changed.

Do you see the difference here? That word *commanded*

in its original text means "constitute." The Bible is more than a collection of principles; it's a heavenly constitution that cannot be changed. Isaiah 40:8 says, *"The grass withers, the flower fades, but the word of our God stands forever"* (NKJV). Jesus repeats this in Matthew 5:18, in which He proclaims, *"For assuredly, I say to you, till heaven and earth pass away, one jot or one tittle will by no means pass from the law till all is fulfilled"* (NKJV).

Guys, we must get this truth into our soul. A popular statement that has surfaced over the last decade about the authority God our King has in His constitution is "God said it, and that settles it, whether I believe it or not."

God gave Adam his first command to follow. He essentially said, "Adam, it will cost you nothing at all to partake of every tree that brings good health to you. But do not, I mean **do not**, partake of the tree that is very cunning, which provides you the extreme of favor, sweets, and wealth or the extreme of sorrow, affliction, mischief, hurt, distress, and misery. Now, if you don't adhere to My constitution, then in that age—in time and in space—you will surely be destroyed." That is our extended, paraphrased version of Genesis 2:16–17.

Very simply, God knew boundaries would be good for the man. He could eventually teach the woman this so they would flourish and prosper in their new kingdom. However, as we all know now, that idea did not go as planned. Eve lusted over the forbidden fruit with eyes and flesh, which was idolatry. It overwhelmed her, so she gave the fruit to man and they both ate, bringing death upon themselves.

A lot of people blame Eve for the fall of man, but it was actually the man who did not display strength to teach the woman to obey God's law. We see that God did not come when Eve ate fruit but, rather, when Adam ate the fruit (Genesis 3:1–10). Yes, she knew the law, but she did not gain the revelation to obey. Think about this: if Adam and Eve had never eaten from the tree of the knowledge of good and evil, that law would still be here today. God's law does not change!

This chapter is not to delve into the fall of man. So we will stop the story there. However, I must reiterate that God has given us a constitution, with principles to help us stay within certain boundaries, so that we can live freely in His kingdom and be completely single, devoted to Him.

I will say this again: **God's laws are good, and His boundaries are necessary to live this life.**

Furthermore, we saw in the first chapter of this book

the importance of dying to your flesh and surrendering it fully to God. Now, in this chapter we will learn how these principles help us control the flesh so we will not cause strongholds of sin to develop in our lives and the lives of those around us.

What Boundaries?

Well, first we have to understand something—that there is absolutely no temptation from which we can't escape. The notion of irresistible temptation is a lie from the pits of hell. 1 Corinthians 10:13 tells us plainly, *"No temptation has overtaken you except such as is common to man; but God is faithful, who will not allow you to be tempted beyond what you are able, but with the temptation will also make the way of escape, that you may be able to bear it"* (NKJV).

God always gives us an escape out of tempting situations. However, if we continuing yielding to sin, we are more than likely going to develop what Paul called a *"seared conscience"* in 1 Paul 4:2.

Let me give you an example of the boundaries God has developed in me. In the fall of 2014, I heard about a movie with a lot of actors I have enjoyed watching over the years, and I thought it would be a good idea to go see it. Now, I had heard only a little bit about the movie. I can honestly say, I didn't do a great job of researching what the movie was about or looking at the comments of recent movie-goers who had already watched the film. This was my mistake, and I'll tell you why.

Within seconds of the film appearing on the big screen, a litany of curse words darted out of the mouths of everyone in that scene. I felt like I was getting punched in the gut every time. Within thirty minutes into the film, the Holy Spirit started saying, "I'm getting vexed, I'm getting vexed, I'm getting vexed," over and over and over. I tried to come back with, "What about my five dollars?" but His words overpowered my small claim.

Do you know what? I just got up and left. I decided it was not worth the two or three months of struggling with cursing that could be rooted in my heart. This could set me back and distract me from focusing on the will of the Father. Since then, I have been even more cautious about what I watch. I have had to turn off certain movies and other entertainment, and I have repented for watching way too long in some cases. It's a process, but it's worth it to stay pure before God!

Ephesians 4:30 states, *"And do not grieve the Holy Spirit of God, by whom you were sealed for the day of redemption"* (NKJV). Or in other words, do not bring sorrow, heaviness, frustration, grief, or vexation to the Holy Spirit.

The Holy Spirit is given to us as gift from Jesus. The Holy Spirit is widely known as our Help, and another of His names is *"the Counselor"* (John 14:26). A counselor is a person trained to give guidance on personal, social, or psychological problems—and the Holy Spirit is literally here to guide us every day.

However, meditating on this on a human level, the people who frustrate me the most are the people with whom I have the closest relationships. Likewise, I believe the disconnect we see appearing in the body of Christ is the lack of relationship with the Spirit. I believe a sad revelation we see today of the Holy Spirit is this: He seems more the third "Power" of the Trinity than the third Person of the Trinity. Yet I am here to say, based not only on my limited knowledge of the Scriptures but also on my personal relationship and experience with Him, that He is a Person and should not be overlooked or ignored any longer.

In Paul's second letter to the church of Corinth, he left them with this salutation: *"The grace of the Lord Jesus Christ, and the love of God, and the **communion** of the Holy Spirit be with you all. Amen."* (2 Corinthians 13:14 NKJV).

The word *communion* holds many meanings, but John Bevere, author of *The Holy Spirit: An Introduction,* gives us three definitions of communion that really stand out in this verse. The Greek word for *communion* is **koinonia**, which means "fellowship, partnership and close mutual association." The one definition I briefly want to touch on is "partnership." Jesus didn't send the Holy Spirit just to show that He has power but, rather, to show He can be a partner. Partners communicate with each other. Look at businesses: usually partners in business do not make a big decision without coming together and agreeing on a resolution.

One of the greatest opportunities to help us stay within boundaries is to develop a true relationship with the Holy Spirit. If you have accepted Jesus as your Lord and are filled with the Spirit, then start speaking to the Holy Spirit to develop that relationship. Do a word search in the Bible and find out the attributes of the Holy Spirit to get to know Him. Speak to Him when you wake up. Ask Him questions with which you are struggling. Just be quiet and listen. Turn off your radio in the car and simply talk to Him—and then listen. This will definitely help you stay within boundaries because you will start feeling what we call a "check" in your spirit when a boundary is being tested.

Loving Jesus is another way to stay within boundaries. Jesus proclaims in John 14:15, *"If you love Me, keep My commandments"* (NKJV). He goes on to say in verse 21, *"He who has My commandments and keeps them, it is he who loves Me. And he who loves Me will be loved by My Father, and I will love him and manifest Myself to him"* (NKJV). So this means, very simply, we cannot proclaim we love Him or have received the full revelation of God's love if we don't follow His commandments. That's the truth.

There are many commandments found in the Bible: those given to us by Moses in the Old Testament, those given to us by the disciples, and those given to us by Jesus. However, Jesus simplifies the matter in His response to a group of Pharisees who were trying to test Him. When one lawyer asked Jesus, "Which is the great commandment in the law?" He replied in Matthew 22:37–40, *"'You shall love the Lord your God with all your heart, with all your soul, and with all your mind.' This is the first and great commandment. And the second is like it: 'You shall love your neighbor as yourself.' On these two commandments hang all the Law and the Prophets"* (NKJV).

Here I ask you to pray this simple prayer I pray often: "Lord God, give me eyes to see what You see. Give me a heart to feel what You feel. Let me love what You love and hate what You hate. Amen." I'm telling you, when you start making this your prayer, you will not have to try to be legalistic and remember all the commandments or laws found in the Bible. Instead, your focus will be on loving people through the eyes of Christ. Yes, you might fall and briefly break a fleshly boundary, but you will soon return to the cross because you are reminded daily what Jesus died for.

One of the last things I personally use to stay within boundaries is wise human counsel. I am going to list a few scriptures from Proverbs that speak on the importance of counsel. Then I will give you a couple of examples of some advice I received from my counsel, to which I try to adhere so I will stay within boundaries and not get hurt.

> *Where there is no counsel, the people fall; but in the multitude of counselors there is safety.* (Proverbs 11:14 NKJV)

> *The way of a fool is right in his own eyes, but he who heeds counsel is wise.* (Proverbs 12:15 NKJV)

> *Listen to counsel and receive instruction, that you may be wise in your latter days.* (Proverbs 19:20 NKJV)

> *He who trusts in his own heart is a fool, but whoever walks wisely will be delivered.* (Proverbs 28:26 NKJV)

You see that wise counsel is beneficial to your success in

this walk, especially with Christ. As we saw in chapter two, the three things by which we all are tempted are the lust of the flesh, lust of the eyes, and the pride of life. So, what have I learned about going on the offensive against the enemy's schemes, which are aimed at preventing me from staying within my boundaries?

What I know about staying within boundaries is that it's all about intentionality. Especially in relationships, boundaries are to be practiced intentionally to prevent both parties from being hurt and to protect the relationship. They are here to protect you—not to keep you from being cool! With that in mind, below are some examples of boundaries for us. As you mature in your relationship with God and with others, you will start setting boundaries up for yourself to combat lust and pride in areas in which you know you are weak.

Boundaries for the Flesh

- If you struggle with pornography, you should put blocks on your computers, laptop, and TV that prohibit access to these sites; or otherwise limit your online browsing behind closed doors.

- Avoid reading sexual-fantasy novels or looking at magazines that may contain nudity, or even partially dressed men or women.

- Avoid engaging in premarital sex, sexting, or masturbation. (See Ephesians 5:3–4 and Matthew 5:27–28.)

- Try to avoid giving the opposite sex full-frontal hugs if you struggle with the spirit of lust. Stick to high-fives, handshakes, and half-hugs, or what we call "church hugs."

- Avoid kissing the opposite sex on the lips if you are not married. (We suggest the forehead or cheek.) Now, if you are weak in this area, refrain from kissing at all.

- Dress appropriately so you don't cause your brother or sister to stumble or fall. (See 1 Corinthians 8:12–13.)

- Avoid dating or courting married people. This can lead to adultery. (Yet people really think this is acceptable for some reason.)

- Don't stay alone with the opposite sex for more than ten to twenty minutes max at a time. Make sure the door is open as well. And yes, that means it is unwise to cohabitate with the opposite sex. (See 2 Timothy 2:22–24.)

- Don't text, video chat, or talk on the phone late. Set a curfew, such as 11 p.m. or midnight. (This is a tough one, and I personally have an accountability partner with whom I check in to make sure I stay in line.)

• *Fast and pray!*

Boundaries for the Eyes

• Avoid looking at pornography in movies, on the Internet, or in books, for you may covet a woman or man with your eyes.

• Avoid extended browsing of social media, as you may become jealous or envious of friends and their lifestyles. Remember, comparison is the enemy to contentment.

• Avoid long periods of time window-shopping in malls, on online stores, or on sites like Amazon, Pinterest, and eBay, which could cause you to start loving material things more and more.

• Limit your viewing of reality TV shows, for you may become dissatisfied with your own life. I don't think they are all bad; however, when you start to compare yourself to the people in such shows, it's probably a good idea to find something else to watch.

• Remember to tithe and to give your offering to

combat the love of money.

- *Fast and pray!*

(Note: Lust of the eyes may lead to a strong desire or compulsion to steal from God and others!)

Boundaries for Pride of Life

- Listen more than you speak. (See James 1:19.)

- Seek to understand before being understood. (See Proverbs 4:7.)

- Seek to find a place to serve in your local church or in your community.

- Praise and worship God at every opportunity. For example, you can play praise and worship music in your car or in your bedroom.

- Work unto the Lord. (See Colossians 3:23.)

- Read and study God's word. (See Joshua 1:8 and 2 Timothy 2:15.)

- *Fast and pray!*

As you see, I added fasting to every category because it disciplines us and keeps us humble. Along with fasting, we should follow Paul's command to *"pray without ceas-*

ing," which we find in 1 Thessalonians 5:17. This will help you tremendously during the tough times in your walk with Christ. Following most of these boundaries, and falling a few times, has helped me strive to become completely single and also stay a virgin.

Yes, that's right, as a thirty-year-old male (at the time of writing this), I can say I am a virgin. In a world that treats sex as an object, I have made a personal decision to accept a new set of eyes and a new heart. I still believe sex is a gift for marriage. I pray you, too, will make this declaration for yourself now. As we will see in the next section, doing so will keep you from a lot of potential trouble in life.

From Boundaries to Bondages

Now, I have to be realistic here. I know that some readers have gone through some tough times before ever knowing about this book. So, what does that mean? Well, on this journey to become #CompletelySingle, we have to be honest with ourselves as well. Before you go on and continue reading, I want you to pray that the Holy Spirit starts highlighting things that might be holding you back from being completely single and, more importantly, from becoming completely free.

You see, the fact is, if we continue to barge through

boundaries, no matter who we are, we more than likely will end up bound by the enemy or in bondage to spiritual forces (Matthew 12:28–29). Others like our parents, friends, families, or associates, could have broken through their own boundaries, bringing these bondages on themselves and on us. This is not your fault; however, we have to expose these areas, acknowledge that they are a real threat, and take authority in Jesus' name.

Let me illustrate what I mean. I believe God provided me this illustration, called "**Bound by the Pound**":

Do you or a friend have a dog? Owners of dogs usually have a fence in the back of the yard so the dog can roam freely. What happens when that dog gets loose? Well, that dog is now in a dangerous situation, and a neighbor can call the pound to capture the dog. And pounds do not discriminate, either! If there is a threat, the pound is sent to catch the dog to protect the other citizens. The reality is that the longer the dog is loose, the more likely the pound will be called to capture the dog.

You see, what the Spirit of the Lord reminded me is that if the dog does get bound by the pound, the only person who has the authority and right to free the dog from the pound's oppression is the owner. No one else can free that dog but the owner. The owner presents the proper documentation to free the dog and then takes it back home to roam in freedom again—within its fence or boundary in the backyard, as intended in the first place.

The fence is our boundaries, the pound is the enemy, and Jesus is the owner. No matter if you are a believer in Christ or not, from this example you can see that if you break out of boundaries in your life, you are more vulnerable to becoming bound if you do not quickly return to your owner, Jesus.

Equally, in this next section we are going to dive into your history a little bit as we start asking you reflective questions. Now, the purpose here is not to highlight areas in your life to show you something's wrong with you. My goal here, rather, is to show you that you are not alone. However, I must also add that not everyone is in bondage, has a stronghold, or is demonized, either. That's very important to recognize early. The following section may just be informational and a reference for some of you to help your friends or family—or even yourself, later on—through trials. Therefore, please take a second and say a quick prayer, asking God to reveal whatever He wants you to gain or deal with today, and also to comfort you as we start this process.

Bondages

Now that you have prayed, and I trust that you have done so, a serious question you might need to ask yourself in this section is: "Why do I keep breaking the boundaries and running from self-discipline and self-control?"

The Bible is clear in Ephesians 6:12, *"For we do not wrestle against flesh and blood, but against principalities, against powers, against the rulers of the darkness of this age, against spiritual hosts of wickedness in the heavenly places"* (NKJV). Therefore, there might be some serious spiritual attacks causing you to fall continually into habitual sin.

One of the purposes of this book is to uncover some of these things that might be causing you to have a debauched relationship with God, first of all, then with yourself, and lastly with others. I personally had to realize the need to look at myself and my history before I pointed the finger accusingly at others for why I may experience terrible relationships.

A major relationship flaw I see occasionally among believers is breaking promises and vows with God Himself, which Ecclesiastes 5:4–5 warns us against. Character weaknesses like these, without true repentance, can cause us to fall and can also open doors to spiritual attack, bondages, or even demonization. No matter if you are male or female, you are a target for the enemy's plan to kill, steal, and destroy your life.

What are some other open doors to bondages?

- Un-confessed sin and yielding to sin

- Pride

- Anger, bitterness, fear, or unforgiveness

- Doubt or unbelief

- False religions

- Involvement in the occult, divination, or horoscopes (astrology)

- Fortune tellers

- Abandonment

- Abortion

- Abusive childhood

- Sickness

- Esteem issues (Self-esteem)

- Involvement in illicit sexual activity or pornography

- Alcohol, drug, or sex addictions

- Not paying your tithes and offerings to your home church

These certain opened doors may lead to depression, oppression, and obsession. You may also feel that you are being harassed or tormented by something and you don't know what it is. Or you may have compulsive tendencies and feel powerless or experience a loss of control in certain areas of your life.

So, how do you know you may need deliverance? How do you know you may have a stronghold? Ask yourself these questions prayerfully:

Do I get sick often? Not all sicknesses are because you are demonized. You might have personally broken natural laws of eating the wrong things, or it could be chastisement (Acts 12:23).

Do I have fits of rage? Not all fits of rage or anger are caused by demonic influences. It could be a lapse in judgment or a case in which the flesh was weak.

Does my competitiveness lead to being over-prideful or to rage?

Am I accident-prone?

Do I have a hard time keeping friends?

Do I have a hard time sleeping or resting?

Do I have an extremely hard time keeping a job?

Do I feel lazy all the time?

Do I have split personalities?

Do I have psychic ability?

Do I hear voices?

Do I have suicidal thoughts?

Do I hate being touched by people?

Do I like to stay isolated or alone for weeks at a time?

Do I have a learning disability?

Did my mother try to abort me?

Was I adopted, and do I feel anger against my birth parents?

When I am dating or courting a person, do I continue to hear my parents correcting me?

Can I not forgive my father or mother for verbally, sexual-

ly, relationally, emotionally, or physically abusing me?

Do I seem unable to shake my addiction to pornography, alcohol, or food?

Do I have demonic or lustful dreams constantly?

Do I have an unusual urge to be naked or expose myself?

Do I have an urge to cheat on my partner?

Do I have an unusual affection for animals?

Do I feel ugly and unattractive?

Do I stare in the mirror? Women: Do I wear too much makeup?

Do I slander others' character?

Do I lie for no reason?

Do I enjoy self-mutilation?

Do I feel a need to drink blood?

Do I hate other races or ethnic groups?

Do I church hop? Am I unable to find a church I like?

Am I over-religious?

Am I a workaholic?

Am I afraid of authority?

Do I have a hard time with my thought life?

This is a relatively short list of things that may be hindering you from moving forward. I have operated in the ministry of deliverance for some time now and have myself been freed from some of these things; and I must say, to be delivered from them is a wonderful place to be. I know one of the initial steps in becoming free is to acknowledge that you are bound. If you have feelings that you are stuck, or you continue in a cycle that you cannot get out of, you are probably in bondage. How do we get out of these bondages?

Or a better question is: How do we overcome demonic attack? Revelation 12:11 says, *"And they overcame him by the blood of the Lamb and by the word of their testimony, and they did not love their lives to the death"* (NKJV).

I have to be perfectly honest with you. Because of what Christ did on the cross (Colossians 2:14–15), the name of Christ (Matthew 10:1, Acts 5:16) and the power of the Holy Spirit (1 John 4:4) will help deliver you from the bondages that are tormenting you. If that was not encouraging enough for you, Jesus stated in Luke 4:18, *"The Spirit of the Lord is upon Me, because He has anointed Me to preach the gospel to the poor; He has sent Me to heal the brokenhearted, to proclaim liberty to the captives and recovery of sight to the blind, to set at liberty those who are oppressed...."* He has come to set the captives free. Hallelujah!

In short, there are typically three ways we instruct individuals to seek help if they're bound: Pray it out, fast it out, or praise it out.

You may need a minister who operates in this ministry often to help you go through a deliverance session and "pray it out," which is more for extreme cases. Ask your local church if there is such a person who operates in this ministry often. If you are a believer in Jesus Christ, however, you should be able to walk someone through the process of deliverance. Mark 16:17–18 encourages believers that they can do this, for as Jesus says, *"And these signs will follow those who believe: In My name they will **cast out demons**; they will speak with new tongues; they will take up serpents; and if they drink anything deadly, it will by no means hurt them; they will lay hands on the sick, and they will recover"* (NKJV).

This chapter only gives us a bird's eye view of spiritual warfare. There are several books on this subject that will help you learn the tactics of the enemy and prepare you for battle. Pastor John Eckhardt's books are a great place to start.

Other than having a minister pray with you, another way to break the chains of bondages in your life is to fast. The last way is to enter into praise and worship with God. Please refer back to chapter 2 on what each of these activities looks like.

But I do want to reiterate here that we can talk about being set free all day long; however, our goal for you is to remain free from bondages. One must repent and confess Jesus Christ as Lord over one's life. He is the only One who can keep the enemy out. Now, if you are not saved and have been delivered, the Bible says in Matthew 12:43–45 that the enemy will go temporarily, but soon will return with seven more wicked demons to reside within you. This is a very serious subject. God wants us saved to protect us and, more importantly, to live with us through eternity. However, whether we are saved or not, breaking through boundaries opens us up for this attack!

Finally, Chip Ingram's series on prayer, titled The Invisible War, gives us a more detailed snapshot of the steps to deliverance. Take some time to read and study the scriptures below as well. Doing so will be beneficial whether you are struggling with bondages or know others who might have shown signs of a struggle themselves.

Steps to Deliverance

1. Unbelievers need to accept Christ. We must admit that we need Jesus! (John 1:12)

2. Believers confess sins. (1 John 1:9)

3. Renounce the works of the devil. (2 Corinthians 4:2)

4. Destroy occult objects—idols and statues. (2 Chronicles 14:2–4, 23:17)

5. Break friendships with occultists, including anyone who subscribes to a system of belief outside of the word of God (2 Corinthians 6:14–16). Avoid missionary dating! That is, do not deceive yourself into pursuing a romantic relationship or courtship with someone with the intention of converting that person into a believer.

6. Rest in Christ's deliverance. (Colossians 1:13)

7. Resist the enemy. (James 4:7–10)

- Submit to God.

- Resist the devil.

- Draw near to God.

- Cleanse your hands.

- Purify your hearts from double-mindedness.

- Respond emotionally: God wants us to surrender our emotions to Him.

- Humble yourself: the Lord is near to the broken-hearted.

8. Meditate on and apply the word of God (Ephesians 6:17; Matthew 4:4–11). Fast from media!

9. Engage in corporate prayer. (Ephesians 6:18; Matthew 18:19)

10. If necessary, perform exorcism in the name of Christ. (Acts 16:16–18)

I hope you really take your freedom to heart. I remember after one deliverance session I had with a couple, I asked the young lady how she felt and she gracefully said, "I feel happy." You see, God does not want you to stay in bondage, and the enemy is doing everything in his power to keep you there. Stand up to the enemy's schemes and seek the truth. God desires you to be completely free so you can do the things He has called you to do, which helps move you toward becoming #CompletelySingle!

Bondage-Breaking Prayer

Father,

We praise Your holy name. In the name of Jesus Christ, my Lord, I bind, abort, renounce, denounce, pull down, cast down, cast out, pluck out, curse, and command every stronghold, generation curse, ungodly soul-tie, and unclean and demonic spirit—whether in the spirit realm; in my will, emotions, mind, tongue, sexual character, or body; in the second heaven where Satan roams, in the abyss, in the sea, and under the earth—that is oppressing, harassing, tormenting, or confusing me or causing obsession, double-mindedness, covetousness, compulsion, control, or demonization: Be broke off of me right now in the name of Jesus Christ of Nazareth!

I bind any and all spirits of rejection, stubbornness, death, memories, self-will, worry, gossip, gluttony, greed, passivity, adultery, shame, guilt, unbelief, doubt, lying, phobias, mental illness, escape, loneliness, resentment, mockery, accusation, control, self-deception, insecurity, fantasy, drugs, hurt, trauma, abandonment, depression, infirmity, lawlessness, rebellion, schizophrenia, materialism, vagabond, anger, grief, fear, lust, homosexuality, addiction, murder, feeling stuck, witchcraft, sexual immorality, the occult, confusion, carnality, jealousy, envy, deception, unforgiveness, selfishness, perversion, bitterness or religious spirits. I curse any remnant of Jezebel, Leviathan, Belial, Behemoth, Baal,

Antichrist, Mammon, Beelzebub, or any chief Marine spirits off of me right now in Jesus' name.

Father, forgive me of my sins of the lust of the flesh, lust of the eyes, and pride of life. I repent right now; I come out of agreement and change my mind about these things. Give me the strength to face my addictions and idols that are keeping me in a habitual cycle to fall into sin. Show me these idols and give me the strength to destroy them and let them go. Father, release me from these bondages right now in Jesus' name!

I pray over all open ports and doors that have been cleaned out by the power of your Holy Spirit. Please fill any open spaces with your gifts and the fruit of the spirit of love, joy, peace, patience, faithfulness, kindness, goodness, gentleness, and self-control. I praise You, Father, for listening to my prayer today and giving us hope! It's in Jesus' name I pray. Amen.

I would continue revisiting this prayer when needed. Repeat over and over until you start seeing true and lasting freedom. Remember, the devil is a liar and the father of lies (John 8:44). Also, note that freedom might take a while or it might be instantaneous. Regardless, continue to seek Jesus, His Cross, and the Holy Spirit!

Reflection Section

_____

_____

_____

_____

_____

_____

_____

_____

_____

_____

_____

_____

_____

"*The meeting of two personalities is like the contact of two
chemical substances: if there is
any reaction, both are trans-
formed.*"

–C. G. Jung

Chapter 5
How to Walk in Divine Purpose

Out of the ground the LORD God formed every beast of the field and every bird of the air, and brought them to Adam to see what he would call them. And whatever Adam called each living creature, that was its name.

— Genesis 2:19 (NKJV)

What Am I Here For?

When I was working as a prayer team leader in 2014, God had me go on a fast in the beginning of the year. I will tell you this was something I did not want to do. I told God I was not going to fast this year; however, the Spirit prompted me to go on a twenty-one-day Daniel fast with my church. I truly believe that because I obeyed the voice of the Lord, He was able to use me for His glory throughout the entire year. I already talked about the benefits of fasting in chapter 2. But now I am going to tell you how this accelerated my divine purpose on the earth.

I was a seasoned prayer team leader with almost a year under my belt, and I felt that I could direct individuals to seek God's face and get results. God wants to work with His children, and He is waiting to unlock something that we need to advance His kingdom here. He will do nothing without our partnership in prayer.

As I started to seek God's face more and more, I saw a trend that God wanted me to keep up, and that was to fast regularly, not just once a year. By my doing this, my sensitivity to the Spirit of God increased—and then something odd started happening. I started to feel the pain and hurts of people around me. It was like I was reading their mail. God was giving me His eyes and His heart for the people around me. I supernaturally saw bondages and strongholds that held people down as well. It was as if I was attracted to hurting people to help them get free.

Then crazy events, which we will call "Bible stuff," started happening. I would pray for people, and they would fall to the ground. And no, I didn't push them. I would lay my hands on the spiritually oppressed, and the demonic would manifest and even speak back to me. People were getting spiritually healed left and right. I even traveled to homes and started praying for my friends and family members, and the same things would happen. Then I felt the Lord say, "This is it." I was operating in the ministry of deliverance.

You see, the word that God gave me in 2014 was "offense." The ministry of deliverance is definitely an offensive, not defensive, calling to deliver people back to the King.

Also in 2014, my publishing company finally trademarked our tag line: "We Deliver Potential." The number fourteen in the Bible means salvation and deliverance. Fittingly enough, in that year God graciously allowed me to step into my divine purpose and calling, and to be a part of delivering people who were eventually restored to the King. Isn't that grand?

Now, as a coach, I have the privilege and opportunity to teach others and to duplicate the person God has created me to be in His kingdom! God has positioned me to become more and more an expert in the ministry so that I don't have to sell myself to the world. However, people come to me because they have heard about the fruit being produced by the Holy Spirit. Trust me: it's not me. It's the Holy Spirit working through me.

I realized have I am nothing without my relationship with God. The late Myles Munroe said, "A fruit tree doesn't take its own fruit off its limbs, go into the stores, and place it on the shelves to be sold. No! A tree that is producing the right fruit will have people come to it and pick its fruit to be distributed." That's my prayer for you—that you'll become so fruitful in your purpose, wherever you are currently planted, that people come to you and send you all over the world to proclaim the glory of the Lord. So let's learn how to live on purpose, becoming fruitful in our singleness to God!

Learning How to Walk in Divine Purpose

When I looked at Genesis 2:19, I didn't immediately get the revelation because I thought it was similar to Genesis 2:15 on the subject of work:

> *Then the Lord God took the man and put him in the garden of Eden to tend and keep it.* (Genesis 2:15 NKJV)

> *Out of the ground the Lord God formed every beast of the field and every bird of the air, and brought them to Adam to see what he would call them. And whatever Adam called each living creature, that was its name.* (Genesis 2:19 NKJV)

But then I slowed down and really focused on what happened in this part of the story. You see, some time had passed, and Adam was learning how to work—to be a great steward of what God had commanded him to do and care for in the garden. When Adam showed faithfulness with his work, God granted Him more responsibility in naming the animals. This is key in our lives as well. Be faithful with the responsibility you currently have first, and God will add more to you!

Two words that really jumped out at me toward the end of the story were the words *called* and *name*. According to *Strong's Concordance*, the word *called* here, in the original text, means to pronounce, call out, publish, mention, meet, and encounter. The word *name* indicates character, authority, and individuality; it means to mark, ordain, and purpose someone or something.

We can see now that Adam was tasked with something greater than work. One could say that this was more like a divine calling. This calling was Adam's territory and domain, and God gave him the authority to name every animal in the Garden. No one else was present. How powerful is this! God gives each of us specific territories to rule and reign over, and in which to have dominion to name things.

Hypothetically, let's add one more person to the story: Eve. What do you think would happen if God tasked both Adam and Eve with naming the animals? Adam and Eve had their own separate mental ability, free will, and capacity for choice given to them by God. I bet, and I am not a betting man, that nine times out of ten, they would both have named the animals totally different names, right?

Now, let me interject something here. Even though

we have choices, the God of the universe who created language and thought is big enough to align certain things so we could speak and name animals similarly. However, there still could be the possibility of each human naming the animals differently. I can only imagine an argument ensuing between Adam and Eve as they were trying to name the animals. Can you hear it, too?

"That doesn't look like a chicken, Adam. It will be called duck."

"No, Eve! Let's call it a butterfly."

"God, who is this woman You hath given me?"

It might have been a big mess.

All jokes aside, I am here to tell you that God has given man a great gift to call out the things that are not as though they are—an authority that Paul attributes to God Himself in Romans 4:17. This is very important to learn as a single person who is seeking to be completely single in His kingdom. Your words have power. Proverbs 18:21 tells us, *Death and life are in the power of the tongue, and those who love it will eat its fruits*" (ESV). When you are walking in your divine purpose and ministry, in the territory God has assigned to you as a leader, you will have the ability to call out different situations and people and put them in their places.

You must quickly figure out who the people are within your ministry and position them accordingly to protect yourself from falling. We will learn later in this chapter that ministry doesn't necessarily have to mean the actual church, either.

Trusting God's Promises

The story of Hagar in Genesis 16 (please read this short story before continuing) is a perfect picture of what we see with men today **forfeiting their promise for something less promising.** You see, in chapter 15, God had promised Abram in a vision that the steward of the house, Eliezer of Damascus, would not be the heir of Abram's house. No, God had promised Abram that even in his old age, he would have a son of his own who would give rise to a great nation.

However, the story takes a turn for the worse in chapter 16. After Abram believed God, Sarai (Sarah) was frustrated because time continued to move on and they did not yet see or understand God's promise. So Sarai devised her own plan and suggested that Abram sleep with her maidservant Hagar, taking her as his concubine (or one-night stand) to fulfill God's promise. The Bible goes on to say after living in the land of Canaan for ten years, Abram went and laid with Hagar the servant, who was not his wife. Abram had a son at eighty-six years of age. His name was Ishmael—and the rest is history.

I want to point out three important things I see in this story to help those who are currently in ministry stay focused and completely single, wholly devoted to God:

1. **The customary thing** – Sarai suggested the customary thing. In the land of Ur of the Chaldeans, their original home, it was customary for men to take a concubine when the wife could not bear any children. This does not make what Abram did right.

   As we apply this to our lives, make sure you are not doing the common thing simply because the world is doing it. Today having sex or living together before marriage is the customary thing even in the church. Here we need to have discipline to follow the commandments and stay within our boundaries so we don't get hurt. After moving into our ministry or proverbial promised land, we must not take the mindset of the old land with us. We must renew our minds daily, as Romans 12:2 teaches us, so we won't fall into old sins. Lastly, we must not forfeit our future for a good thing but, rather, seek out the God thing in every area of our lives.

2. **Ten years** – Did you catch that? Abram lived in

the land of Canaan for ten years before he lay with Hagar. In the Bible numbers are very important. The number ten represents testing or trial.

How did I catch this number? Well, God is so awesome. Before the beginning of the year 2015, I was praying to God on how long I should fast. Over the last couple of years, our church has participated in a corporate fast. I heard the number ten when I prayed to God, but I wanted to make sure it was the Lord and not my flesh—because I like to eat a lot. My confirmation came when I came across Daniel 1:14–15, which says, *"So he consented with them in this matter, and tested them ten days. And at the end of ten days their features appeared better and fatter in flesh than all the young men who ate the portion of the king's delicacies"* (NKJV).

I really started writing the majority of this book during that ten-day fast. The number ten was highlighted for me throughout that fast, so as soon as I read it in this story of Abram, Sarai and Hagar, the number ten leaped off the page. However, I may have missed this important number if God had not already highlighted it for me before my fast even started. God works in mysterious ways doesn't He?

How many plagues were there? Ten. How many

commandants did Moses write down? Ten. And how much is the tithe that we are instructed to bring to God? Ten percent. Abram was being tested in his tenth year in his promised land and tried by the Most High God, and he failed. I pray you recognize the test in your life today. I heard a pastor say once, "The teacher doesn't talk during the test." Is this your testing year? God is teaching you something. Hold on to His promises. I pray that the men and women to whom you are supposed to minister would not distract you! I pray that you would be found faithful against and amongst the crowd.

3. **Do you really trust Him?** – I know a lot of people would say they would never do what Abram did, but I would be truthful and say I don't know if I would have trusted God, either. Who knows what I would have done under those circumstances? We sometimes look at Abram's and Sarai's story, pointing the finger at Abram and saying the adultery was the only major sin here. Yes, adultery or taking in a concubine is terribly wrong, but the bigger sin here is that Abram did not teach Sarai the importance of what it meant to go against God's word and what that would ultimately mean for their family. As Hosea 4:6 says, our people *"are destroyed from lack of knowledge"* (NIV).

We see the same thing with Adam and Eve: the major sin here is doubt and unbelief. If God tells you something about your future, purpose, calling, or ministry, believe it. Do you really trust God that He will provide you with a spouse (to the singles), provide you the provision you seek, or even satisfy your every desire? Really, search your heart here. This is something I had to come to grips with and repent over when I started focusing on my present situation as a single male. We have to stay in the word of God often and keep the faith. Contact your close friends and ask them to keep you accountable with your thought life as well.

We see that because of what Abram did, not trusting God, the world has been affected by the seed of Hagar. The angel of the Lord told Hagar to name her son Ishmael because he would be a *"wild man"* and *"his hand shall be against every man, and every man's hand against him"* (Genesis 16:12 NKJV). We see this today. The descendants of Ishmael and the descendants of Isaac, whom we now know as Israel, are fighting against each other still to this day.

For your part, your ministry is the people in your current circle, as Sarai was in Abram's circle. This can be your family members whom you have the opportunity to point toward and reconcile back to God. However, we tend to try to reconcile people back to ourselves instead, as if we are gods. That's why we have to be very careful not to manipulate individuals to fill our personal voids or satisfy our flesh while we are doing the will of the Father. We see this happening all the time in both the world and the body of Christ. It must stop!

Why Am I Here?

Our true purpose comes in knowing Jesus Christ and His plan for our lives. We find three foundational keys to help us with our purpose for existence that Jesus laid out for us. Here they are:

Mission

> *And Jesus came and spoke to them, saying, "All authority has been given to Me in heaven and on earth. Go therefore and make disciples of all the nations, baptizing them in the name of the Father and of the Son and of the Holy Spirit, teaching them to observe all things that I have commanded you; and lo, I am with you always, even to the end of the age" Amen.* (Matthew 28:18–20 NKJV)

If you call yourself a disciple of Jesus Christ and said "yes" to Him, you are looking at your **mission statement:** "Go make a disciple." That's it. That's our mission. A scary statistic I heard from a ministry called

Downline Ministries, which focuses on discipleship, said that according to one of their studies, less than two percent of the church has caught the vision of being obedient to this commandment to disciple other people. However, this will not be you. Since you were discipled, seek to make disciples. But how do you find a disciple like you?

- **Pray!** I believe the first thing we need to do is involve God the Father, His Son, and His Spirit. For example, spend some time in devotion with the Trinity, seeking out the person(s) God wants you to pour your life into. Maybe this person is right under your nose and you don't even realize it. As a disciple, you are looking for what Dawson Trotman from the Navigators calls *F.A.T.* individuals: "Faithful, Available, and Teachable."

- **Study sound doctrine!** I have to be completely honest with you: we can't be disciples of Christ and not know what He says. We also can't communicate Jesus' teachings to others. We need to live His word out actively in our lives.

- **Take the make-up off!** I say this often: people want to follow real people. Don't be fake! If God is prompting you, be willing to show some of your battle wounds from past situations that God has helped you through. This gives your disciples a great reference point to recall if he or she ever goes through a similar experience. Spend time with these people. Go out for meals. Show them how you share the gospel with unbelievers and believers. Show them how you interact with your wife or husband, your friends, and your family members. Just be real.

- **Start with where someone is!** Everyone is made different—that's a fact. We all go through different situations and experience a variety of circumstances that shape our realities. So I believe we can learn from Jesus, who met His disciples where they were in life. He talked to them about things they were familiar with. For example, He used parables about fishing and farming to teach His followers about the kingdom of God. We should ask God to give us a teaching spirit to meet our disciples the same way.

Finally, my friends, a fruit is not a fruit unless its seed is producing fruit. The same is true with discipleship. A disciple cannot be called a disciple unless his or her disciples are discipling! (See Matthew 10:7–8 and Mark 16:17–18.)

Ministry

Therefore, if anyone is in Christ, he is a new creation; old things have passed away; behold, all things have become new. Now all things are of God, who has reconciled us to Himself through Jesus Christ, and has given us the ministry of reconciliation, that is, that God was in Christ reconciling the world to Himself, not imputing their trespasses to them, and has committed to us the word of reconciliation.

Now then, we are ambassadors for Christ, as though God were pleading through us: we implore you on Christ's behalf, be reconciled to God. For He made Him who knew no sin to be sin for us, that we might become the righteousness of God in Him.
(2 Corinthians 5:17–21 NKJV)

As this scripture so beautifully explains, when we accept salvation, we are reconciled back to God through the sacrifice of Jesus Christ. Our ministry is to go into the entire world and help reconcile the lost, as we were lost, back to God. No matter what industry we are in. When we start realizing this culture of discipleship and reconciliation, families and nations will be radically changed. Prayerfully, these groups will start following suit and start to be reconciled back together. We all need to pray for God's eyes of compassion and love, like Christ, so we can start walking in this divine ministry.

Message

> *From that time Jesus began to preach and to say, "Repent, for the kingdom of heaven is at hand"* (Matthew 4:17 NKJV).

> *Thy kingdom come. Thy will be done in earth, as it is in heaven* (Matthew 6:10 KJV).

What's our message to the people? That the kingdom of God is here.

The kingdom of God is found in the Holy Spirit and is manifested when we become born again. Romans 14:17 says, "...*for the kingdom of God is not eating and drinking, but righteousness and peace and joy in the Holy Spirit*" (NKJV). We have to get this. That's why it is so important to seek a relationship with the Holy Spirit. However, the enemy is working overtime in distorting your understanding of the Holy Spirit because once you get this message down, that the kingdom of God is here, oh man—he is doomed. So getting to know the Spirit of God and this message, along with your testimony, will be that much more powerful.

How Do I Find My Divine Purpose or Calling?

Great question! Now you know that we all have the same mission, ministry, and message. However, where you're specifically placed on the earth and how the message is delivered are what I see a lot of people struggle with. This section will help you grasp your specific calling.

That said, I must tell you that everybody is different and people discover their divine purpose or call at different times in their life. However, if you currently don't know what you are divinely called to do, the first suggestion I would give you is not to get discouraged.

The following points are additional suggestions for you to consider in seeking your divine purpose or calling. Again, be patient with the process. If you start implementing these suggestions, I am confident that you will start developing a picture and portrait of what you are here for!

Pray

I know you are saying, "Man, Damien wants me to pray a lot!" Yes, that's the key. The Bible tells us again in Thessalonians to *"pray without ceasing."* I believe it's imperative to live a life of prayer and seek God whenever you are trying to look for purpose in Christ and where He wants you positioned. One realization the Lord gave me as I was meditating is that there are certain people who are in the wrong place and, therefore, they are growing at the wrong pace. Yes, God works everything together for our good when we love Him, but there is nothing like seeing a person in the right position, serving and growing in his or her purpose. You can definitely tell the difference.

Your prayer here should be, "Lord, You have given me a mission, ministry, and message. Now, in what industry do you want me to be, Lord? Amen." The misconception here is that we all have to be in church to be effective, and that's not true. On average, we are only at church one to two days a week for just a few hours. The rest of our time is spent at work and home. So maybe, just maybe, our calling is in those two places first! Further, one could even argue that your family is your first ministry—so start there.

Write Your Story

That's right: Start writing your autobiography. This is a wonderful exercise you can do today. Begin with your earliest memory and write all the events in chronological order. Write out the good times, the bad times, and even the traumatic times. Then highlight all the events that were traumatic; see how you reacted to each and how it has shaped your life. See also if there are certain themes connecting the different traumatic events.

Additionally, you can start writing what you think your future will hold. What would you like to be doing in the next five to ten years? See if there is anything in your past that is also highlighted in your future. This may be your divine calling.

Use Your Gifts and Talents

What are you gifted at? James 1 tells us that every good and perfect gift comes from above. So we must first recognize that our gift or talent is not ours for us to keep and hide. It must be given away—because it's never a gift until it is given away. If money were not an issue, what would you do with your time? What gift or talent comes to you naturally or easily, so much that you don't understand why other people just can't get it like you? This may be your gift that you might want to focus on. Write this gift down and pray to see where God wants you to give your gift and talent to others.

Another misconception is that John Doe's gift has granted him access to worldwide fame; my gift doesn't matter. That is false! Your gift does matter, and you just have to focus on fine-tuning your gift. Other people will start noticing the fruit that you have to offer, which brings glory to our Father. In 1 Corinthians, the Bible tells us that, as believers in Christ, we all belong to the same body—but different parts. If you are a foot, I beg you not to try to be like the ear. Be the best foot you can be!

Now, concerning gifts, there are people who are physically gifted and talented, like basketball players, football players, artists, and musicians. However, when you are baptized with the Holy Spirit, you have access to His gifts. Here is a list of the spiritual gifts given to us from the Holy Spirit.

Administration	Leadership
Apostleship	Mercy
Discernment	Miracle-working
Evangelism	Pastoring/Shepherding
Exhortation	Prophecy
Faith	Serving/Ministering
Giving	Teaching
Healing	Tongues
Interpreting Tongues	Wisdom
Knowledge	

These spiritual gifts are found in Romans 12:6–8, 1 Corinthians 12:8–10 and 28–30, and Ephesians 4:11. We are not going to go over each of these gifts and explain them to you in this book. However, you can go online and take a free test to start seeing how God has wired you in His kingdom (http://www.spiritualgiftstest.com/test/adult).

Be Angry—At the Right Things

Being angry is not a bad thing, even though many people think it is. God has given us this feeling! How you react with the anger that you have is another story. Ephesians 4 instructs us to be angry, but we must not sin. In Matthew 21, we see Jesus got angry in the temple with the moneychangers and drove them out of the temple because they were defiling the Lord's house.

Think about a time when you have noticed some type of injustice in the world. Maybe it's the poor, our youth in prison, or the overall political process. And perhaps when you observed this, you just got mad and said to yourself, "If I were involved, I know something would change." This might be your holy burden, or a place God is calling you to. For me, it was seeing people struggle with different strongholds of sin. I hate being in bondage myself, and I especially hate seeing people I love and others in bondage. Therefore, God gave me a supernatural gift of discerning spirits, and I help people get free from bondage!

So, what is your **holy burden**? What causes righteous anger every time you see injustice?

Volunteer

Another suggestion I have for you is to volunteer. I didn't start serving in the prayer team right away; I started in the children's ministry called "VKids." I love the administrative side of things and how they work, so I volunteered faithfully—I believe for a couple of months—until I got the tug to join the prayer team. However, I had to take a risk first to be led into the right ministry. Many of you are like how I was, and you are just taking up space at your local church, making sure you warm the seat up for the next service. I must tell you to get up out of your seat and volunteer in a ministry!

Look at the shepherd boy David, in 1 Samuel 17. Even as a young adult, he told King Saul that he would volunteer to fight the Philistines, where he eventually faced and slayed Goliath. After several more years, that shepherd boy became a king, and his seed produced Jesus Christ. You see, David just took what he had—three smooth rocks and a slingshot, which was laughable for many to take to a fight against a giant. But we must remember, he used to practice with that slingshot day in and day out. He even had experience with large animals like a bear and a lion. He was more than ready to fight Goliath. He was confident that God gave him enough skill to take on the enemy, and you need to have the same mindset as well.

Like David, you have to practice your gift and ability. I believe God has given you enough skill, ability, gifts, and talents to do so. One thing I do almost every day, if not every day, is practice public speaking, whether it's in the shower, in front of the mirror, or in the car. I recite speeches even though no one is watching. Why? Because there might be a chance for me to get on stage or behind a camera and tell the world who Jesus is one day. I want to prepare myself and try to represent Him the best way I can. One of my late mentors said, "It's better to be prepared and never have a speaking opportunity than not to be prepared but have an opportunity to speak."

Now it's your turn. Take that step of faith and do something with your gift. Even though no one is watching, practice it—and **go** and **volunteer**!

Where do you I start, you ask? Well, Jesus gives us some suggestions in Matthew 25:35–36:

> *For I was hungry and you gave me something to eat, I was thirsty and you gave me something to*

drink, I was a stranger and you invited me in, I needed clothes and you clothed me, I was sick and you looked after me, I was in prison and you came to visit me. (NIV)

Build a Team

One of my last points in this chapter **on finding your divine purpose or calling** is the importance of having an accountability team. I believe this is crucial as you step into the will of God for your life. Also, an accountability team protects you so you don't get filled up with pride and put yourself in compromising situations. Having a group of people holding you accountable, especially as you deal with the opposite sex, is something that has helped me as I strive to be completely single. We have seen so many people fall because they either placed themselves on a pedestal or allowed other people to place them on a pedestal. The next thing you know, the news is broadcasting their fall! Please, take heed to this advice. Surround yourself not with "yes" men and women but with godly people, especially those who have the spiritual gift of wisdom, knowledge, or discernment.

Sleeping with Your Ministry

Before we get started on the meaning of "sleeping with

your ministry," I must say that this is not my original metaphor. I will not take credit for this phrase, as I briefly heard it in a sermon. However, I did pray and meditate on it, and God highlighted one passage in the Bible for me that shows it perfectly: the story of Abram, Sarai, and Hagar, which we read earlier.

This title phrase may be a little strong, yet I believe I am led to write it. If you're living in purpose and on purpose and are completely single, then good. I encourage you to be energized by the rest of this book and, continue to work as unto the Lord, to focus on doing the work of the Lord in the ministry He placed you in, and encourage others in the faith as well. If you are working on being #CompletelySingle, keep on reading. This next section will help you.

Now, what I have seen too many times is that people fall because they could not balance the fifth and sixth principles of this book—living with divine purpose while learning how to rest. These individuals were distracted, not recognizing the schemes and tactics of the enemy. Instead of living a life on the offense, they were getting beat up on the defense, and they started focusing on their loneliness. This in turn caused them to look at every single man or woman who walked across their path. These people they were looking at could have been single, courting someone else, or even married.

If you are at this state in your walk, I am praying that you turn back to the Comforter, the Holy Spirit. However, I wanted to offer you some advice here and encouragement if you are still having trouble.

Men, every woman that is paraded in front of you is not your wife (period). Women, every man in a position of service leadership is not your husband, either. Don't let your friends or family members encourage this behavior: "Aye man, I just met your wife! I don't know what nationality she is, but she might be an angel, bro." Or I have heard women say to their girlfriends, "Girl, that's your husband. You better claim it." Actually, it's witchcraft if you are naming and claiming every "fine" brother (for my sisters in Christ) and "fine" sister (for my brothers in Christ) who walks by you. If you are that friend, I implore you, please, to stop it!

Friends and/or family, what you are doing is causing frustration in a single person's life. You are also creating a spirit of anxiousness in their life when the Bible clearly says to be anxious for nothing, in Philippians 4 verse 6. Even the *single* person can feel inadequate in that area as well. This is very dangerous and can lead the person into a state of shame, resentment, bitterness, unrighteous anger, embarrassment, irritation, restlessness, isolation and ultimately even more seriously depression. Their trust is moving away from God's timing and His will. So again, if you are a friend or family member who has been practicing this behavior, my best advice is to direct them to seek God's face! Yes, it is cool to encourage your friends if they are isolating themselves and not socializing at all, to pursue godly relationships and even marriage. Relating with the opposite sex matures the individual on many levels. However, you should also praise and encourage the person for what they are doing in the kingdom as well. It definitely needs to be a balance.

Now, without the balance of both kinds of encouragement here—toward seeking godly relationships and toward pursuing work in the kingdom—we might continue to see an increase in premature relationships in and out of the church. Commonly, both parties are not mature enough to support the other person spiritually and emotionally, and sadly do not have a clear vision for their relationship. This can lead to someone in the relationship getting hurt and what I have seen even in the church is premature sex which is adultery! Because this book is mainly written to the men, I beseech you my brothers, to stop sleeping with your ministry!

We have a church body filled with sexual immorality and sexual perversion. The body of Christ looks just likes the world with baby mamas and daddies who are unmarried, trying to do the best they can without killing each other. Also, we might even see hints of incest, adultery, sex outside of marriage, and other explicit sexual sin. We even find that the enemy has distorted the thinking of some people in our society to the point that they engage in bestiality or zoophilia—sleeping with animals. Romans 1 warns us of loving the creation more than the Creator and having unnatural relations. We must be very careful not to obtain a debased mind. When we walk with divine purpose, we have to make sure we fall more in **love** with Jesus rather than make the mistake of falling in **lust** with anyone or anything else, including the ministry.

This principle of divine purpose is meant to help you thrive in your purpose and speak eternity into your ministries, not sleep with it! But thank God we have redemption and He forgives our mistakes and blots our transgression. We have to return to Jesus and accept His blood sacrifice for these sins!

Prayer for Purpose

Father, thank You for giving me Your Mission, Ministry and Message to take to the uttermost parts of the world. Please give me direction so I can be in the right position in Your kingdom. Highlight the gifts and talents that I may have overlooked and open up a situation where I can volunteer and use this to impact Your kingdom. It's in Jesus' name I pray. Amen.

Reflection Section

_____

_____

_____

_____

_____

_____

_____

_____

_____

_____

_____

_____

"To be fully seen by somebody, then, and be loved anyhow— this is a human offering that can border on miraculous."

-Elizabeth Gilbert

Chapter 6
How to Rest

And the Lord God caused a deep sleep to fall on Adam,
and he slept…

— Genesis 2:21a (NKJV)

If You Don't Work, Don't Eat

As you can see from the title for this chapter, I am going to talk about resting. But before we talk about rest, I believe we need to talk about the extreme opposite of rest: works and toiling. Today more and more people in the world, and even in the body of Christ, are toiling like never before. What are you trying to achieve? They are burnt out, and you can see it all over their faces. Do you feel burnt out? I mean, are you tired all the time?

Now, don't get me wrong; work is good, as we stated in the stewardship chapter. It produces self-discipline, self-control, and a sense of responsibility. However, there is definitely a difference between work and toil, which is keeping people in general from living a more abundant life. There is a scripture about work in the word of God that I hear misquoted and, I believe, misinterpreted:

For even when we were with you, we command-ed you this: If anyone will not work, neither shall he eat. For we hear that there are some who walk among you in a disorderly manner, not working at all, but are busybodies. Now those who are such we command and exhort through our Lord Jesus Christ that they work in quietness and eat their own bread. (2 Thessalonians 3:10–12 NKJV)

I always heard this as "If I don't work, I am not going to eat," but not the rest of the verse. Because I didn't have a full revelation of this verse, it made me seek work more than I sought after God to supply my needs. My focus was more on surviving than on being sustained by Him. That's where the toil starts creeping in and the love of material things and money (also known as the spirit of Mammon) may find its roots in our lives.

If we look further at this verse, we see who Paul really was concerned about. These people are disorderly, not working much or at all, and busybodies. Are you in any of these categories? If you are **disorderly,** you probably do not possess the fruit of the Spirit. You cause dissension between your co-workers; you are a troublemaker, and soon you may not even have a job to feed yourself or your family because companies are not going to deal with employee conflict or strife.

Are you **not working**? By this I mean, are you unemployed and not *actively* looking for a place to work? If you are actively looking for a job, great! Then this does not apply to you. But if you are not looking for work, you are what the Bible calls slothful and you may be oppressed with a vagabond spirit. Pray and ask God to reveal to you why you are not seeking work.

Lastly, are you a **busybody**? Are you all over the place and lacking any sense of purpose in your life or within your family? Paul was trying to light a fire under people in a specific church who were disorderly, not working at all, or busybodies. If you know of people like this, please pray that God changes their heart. However, this scripture should not be thrown at people to make them feel ashamed and guilt them into a mode of toiling. Instead, they should be accepting the supernatural provision of God's rest!

Learning How to Rest

I am truly excited about this last principle—that of rest. You see, there are numerous believers who stop at the principle of divine purpose as presented in the last chapter. They're not aware of the last test: we must learn how to rest!

We see in Genesis 2:21 that the Lord God caused

Adam to sleep—and he slept. Man, this is powerful. And as I dissected this last principle of being completely single, I noticed something else: in the process of being completely single, God never mentioned women—not even once. Adam was so focused on learning how to live and work, learning God's boundaries and learning His purpose for him, that a need for a woman never crossed his mind. Our gracious Father supplied a wonderful gift, in the form of rest, before the woman ever showed up on the scene.

In the original text, we see that God overwhelmed the man and placed him into a deep trance, where he remained for a very long time. I love the definition that *Strong's Concordance* gives for *slept* or the word *inveterate*: it means to "have a habit or interest that is long-established and unlikely to change."

Now, be honest: In your pursuit of finding a courtship partner or potential spouse, have you considered allowing yourself to be overwhelmed by the peace and rest that the Father offers? Do you have a habit of trusting that the Lord will provide the right spouse for you, or are you too busy making your own plans, even if you claim otherwise? I know this is hard even for me as I type this chapter, but the point is so crucial to hammer home. As I mentioned before, I myself have to repent often for not truly trusting God in this area. If we can be completely honest, maybe our prayer needs to be the one found in Mark 9:24: *"I do believe; help me overcome my unbelief!"* (NIV).

Resting is not being lazy or being a sluggard, which sometimes tend to be associated with it. I would define resting in the Father as "**actively waiting** on God as I am led by the Spirit of God, being found working advancing His kingdom." That's rest! Now, let's look at one area in which we all are subject to fall—busyness.

Being Busy

One of the major tricks of the enemy is to keep you not merely busy, but completely busy. Staying busy gets us out of whack and out of alignment with the word of God, leading us to a shamble-filled life. Just think about a car when it is out of alignment. It affects the whole car, doesn't it? You are pulled slightly to the right or hard to the left. Your tires will even start deteriorating faster than normal. Busyness can also cause deterioration in our relationship with people and, most importantly, our relationship with the Father.

Are you too busy? As you think about that, consider a vision I had in the summer of 2014:

I was driving in a car in the city of Atlanta, looking for a parking spot on the side of the road, but none was available. Then I saw it—a parking garage! I pulled my car in, rolled down the window, and just as I was about to stick my hand out to push the button for a ticket, I noticed something interesting: the arm to let me into the parking garage was raised before I even pushed the button to get my ticket!

A lot of us are in this very same place. *We are trying to pay and work for something to which God has already given us access.* You see, as my revelation continued, the Spirit of God said, "Why are they not pulling into the garage, parking their car, and resting in My presence? They are already in My household, which means I will take care of them and their provisions." Very simply, stop toiling and rest!"

We have to remember that, as believers in Christ, we are in His household, so there is no need for us **not** to rest. Jesus did all the work on the cross, so we can just focus on living for Him and not toiling like slaves to earn His approval. Busyness will cause us to start living by the flesh, or what the Bible calls carnality. We will then have a tough time renewing our minds as we are instructed to do.

Roman 8:5–8 explains this clearly:

> *For **those who live according to the flesh set their***

minds on the things of the flesh, but those who live according to the Spirit, the things of the Spirit. For to be carnally minded is death, but to be spiritually minded is life and peace. Because the carnal mind is enmity against God; for it is not subject to the law of God, nor indeed can be. So then, those who are in the flesh cannot please God. (NKJV)

So you see, the enemy wants to keep you in a state of busyness, focusing on the flesh, which causes carnality. This gets in the way of God teaching us what it means to rest, and of us discovering the peace associated with rest.

Do you see what this can potentially do to us? We can become so busy and worried about working, or about material things, we end up working at a dead-end job. Or we may be so busy that we end up serving in the wrong place in our local church and not discovering our true calling or ministry. We can also be so busy looking at the flesh that we are not in the right position to find people God wants us to meet to advance His kingdom.

Even more tragically, we may be so busy that we marry the wrong person, not the person God intended us to marry. Do you see the implication now of not resting in the Father? Abram didn't pass the test, and it affected the world. Are we going to past the rest test?

So What Do We Do About This?

My friends, we have to find time to rest! God has already given us a guideline in the very beginning, when He rested Himself. We find this in Genesis 2:2–3: *"And on the seventh day God ended His work which He had done, and He rested on the seventh day from all His work which He had done. Then God blessed the seventh day and sanctified it, because in it He rested from all His work which God had created and made"* (NKJV).

As you can see, He sanctified the day, which means He consecrated, dedicated, appointed, purified, and observed it! Now, if God took time from creating and was *"refreshed,"* which Exodus 31:17 tells us, then what is our excuse? Don't become busybodies like the New Testament Christians to whom Paul was talking. You can find time to rest—because it's good and holy.

Now, in the body of Christ, we call this taking a Sabbath day, which comes from the Ten Commandments in the Old Testament. For the Jewish people, the Sabbath was from Friday night to Saturday night. Because of the Catholic influence, this day has changed to Sunday. Nevertheless, as believers in Jesus Christ, we feel that the true Sabbath is in the Person of Jesus Christ, not in a particular day (Hebrews 4).

However, we still believe we are to take one day out of the week and rest. The Sabbath is a gift God gave to the children of Israel after they had been enslaved for more than four hundred years. According to Strong's the word *Sabbath* means to leave, or a cessation of work, exertion, or activity. It also means to celebrate. We are called to celebrate God on our day of rest! He has done so many good things in our lives that He requires us to take one day to do just that. Does this sound great, or what?

I started truly resting and taking my Sabbath when I began faithfully going to my church here in Atlanta, called Victory World Church. I started to see enormous advancements in my emotions, spiritual life, and health. I am now much more jovial of a person, and I don't get rattled easily anymore. I have learned how to rest, which in turn places my trust in the Father to provide for me when I am not working.

I also take sabbaticals, which are longer times of rest. These are typically more extended rest periods when you meet with God and He restores you from any damaged areas that only He can touch. Many pastors and ministers must take sabbaticals, but this practice is hardly exclusive to the ministry.

How Do You Rest?

I have learned three ways to rest: physically, emotionally, and spiritually. I think learning to rest has truly been the catalyst by which God has molded me into the person I am today—and I believe this can be the same for you. God will refresh you like never before!

Physical Rest

Let's start with physical rest. Resting physically is really tough for people these days. I see this even with the young adults I minister to. People have two or three jobs because of family dynamics or situations where there is one provider in the home. Yes, this is unfortunate; however, God is still calling us to find some time for physical rest. If not, we could become ineffective in doing ministry for the kingdom of God, whether it is in our workplaces or church.

Whether you are an athlete, artist, or a blue- or white-collar worker, He is calling you to find time to rest physically. Luke 16:13 says, *"No servant can serve two masters; for either he will hate the one and love the other, or else he will be loyal to the one and despise the other. You cannot serve God and mammon* [money]" (NKJV). Take some time to pray and see if mammon is at the root of you working so much or if you are a workaholic.

Here are some recommendations for your day off: First, do not work at all at your main job, or for your business if you are an entrepreneur. I personally tell clients and those who work with me that Wednesday is my day to rest since I currently work an odd schedule. Do not respond to work emails, work-related text messages, or memos. This also means you should try not to do any major cleanup projects around the house on your day of rest.

My favorite way to think about this is that I am going to be pampered by God today and we are going to celebrate together. I like going out driving and walking. I might catch a movie or visit friends and family. Some people like going on nature trails to pray and talk to the Father. I would advise you not to go on a huge shopping spree only to tire yourself out, which defeats the purpose. On this day it's good to get adequate rest. Sleep in. If you usually get four or five hours of sleep on a regular day, it's all right to get eight hours of sleep on your day of rest. Yes, really! Also, because you are resting, read and study the word of God.

I have received some of my best revelations for my *Thoughts From The Box* devotionals on my day of rest. However, on this day, I have refrained from writing. Instead I have prayed, asking God if He wants me to change anything or add something, and He has instructed me accordingly. I have taken notes, but have not done any serious writing.

Now, I am not insisting that you be legalistic, either. For instance, my natural father asked me to help him move on my Sabbath because his church was transitioning into a new building, and I helped. After all, we see scriptures in which Jesus healed the sick on the Sabbath—we see this in Mark 3:1–6, when Jesus healed a man's withered hand. So if the ministry calls on you, be open to move and be led by the Spirit.

Finally, my friends, Jesus rested; therefore, we must also rest. We saw this when He slept on the boat. If Jesus can find time to sleep, especially in a storm (Mark 4:38), we can find time to sleep as well.

Emotional Rest

Are you emotionally healthy? Really? Emotional health is a vital matter. I personally have to watch my emotional health, and my accountability partners must do the same for me. We see this in relationships all the time: when people who are not emotionally healthy suppress and bottle up their emotions for years but then, one day, just snap! One of the driving forces may be that such people are not resting emotionally.

We all have different emotions attached to us from our childhood experiences, our adult relationships, and our daily life. These things hold us back from really resting, even on our Sabbath day. Unforgiveness and bitterness lay heavily on the church, and I see them rear their ugly heads often. Also, the spirit of rejection, fear, abandonment, and grief tends to keep relationships from ever moving to the next level. We have to be self-aware, and not just talk over our past experiences, because they can shape our future negatively if we don't handle them by applying the word of God.

Don't let the enemy make you fearful of the freedom available to you today when you rest in the Lord. Below are some scriptures you can meditate on as you learn how to rest emotionally in the word of God.

> *Who is slow to anger is better than the mighty, and he who rules his spirit, than he who captures a city.* (Proverbs 16:32 NASB)

> *Let all bitterness, wrath, anger, clamor, and evil speaking be put away from you, with all malice. And be kind to one another, tenderhearted, forgiving one another, even as God in Christ forgave you.* (Ephesians 4:31–32 NKJV)

> *Be anxious for nothing, but in everything by prayer and supplication, with thanksgiving, let your requests be made known to God; and the peace*

of God, which surpasses all understanding, will guard your hearts and minds through Christ Jesus. (Philippians 4:6–7 NKJV)

Which of you by worrying can add one cubit to his stature? (Matthew 6:27 NKJV)

Therefore do not worry about tomorrow, for tomorrow will worry about its own things. Sufficient for the day is its own trouble. (Matthew 6:34 NKJV)

*This is what the LORD says: "Stand at the crossroads and look; ask for the **ancient paths**, ask where the good way is, and walk in it, and you will find rest for your souls. But you said, 'We will not walk in it.'"* (Jeremiah 6:16 NIV)

If you believe you need to be delivered from some emotional things in your past, please refer to chapter 4 or speak to a counselor or minister at your local church. You can also contact the ministry called Ancient Paths, developed by Craig Hill (https://www.craighill.org). This ministry has helped thousands of people get to the root of their emotional pain and has led them to freedom.

As you learn how to rest emotionally in the Father, may the peace of God reign over you!

Spiritual Rest

Matthew 11:28 says, *"Come to Me, all you who labor and are heavy laden, and I will give you rest"* (NKJV). Don't you love Jesus? Even though this scripture is being applied to those who are toiling physically, it has spiritual implications as well. Is your spirit laboring and heavy-laden? Maybe this is a result of your passion for those to whom you are ministering, or perhaps it is because of what everyone struggles with from time to time—sin!

Sin is a word used less and less in churches and other religious gatherings across the world today. The New Testament, in its original text, uses five different terms for sin; I will mention three here. **Hamartia** is a Greek word and the most common usage. A hunting term, it is translated as "missing the mark or target." This means failing to be what we might have been or could have been. As Christians, we believe that sin separates us from God the Father and keeps us from living in eternity with God in heaven. Another term we find in the Greek for *sin* is **anomia**, which means lawlessness. This refers to someone who deliberately breaks the law. And the word **opheiléma** translates as *debt*. A debt here means a failure to pay that which is due—a failure in duty.

True spiritual rest comes with repentance of our sins. Whether we have missed the mark, have broken a law, or are in debt, we must repent and come back to Jesus. As Acts 3:19 puts this, *"Repent therefore and be converted, that your sins may be blotted out, so that times of refreshing may come from the presence of the Lord..." (NKJV)*. Other translations, such as the ESV, use *"turn back"* instead of *"be converted."* True repentance, in short, is much more than saying "I'm sorry." Rather, true repentance is when people turn around—180 degrees—and make a decision to move their mind, their heart, and their body away from the sin and the evil one. Instead, they move toward God, through Jesus.

We just need to change our minds, confess our sins (1 John 1:9), repent, and come back to Jesus, accepting His way and His work that has been finished on the cross! What I have seen in my life and the lives of others around me is that we sometimes stop at the third step—repentance—and think everything is okay, but then we get sucked up back into our sin. I call this stage "second-guessing our mess." We believe our mess will be more fun than God's blessing for our life, and we end up sad, busted, and disgusted! Instead, we need to continue on from repentance to Jesus. Once we do that, spiritually, we can rest in the Father's rest!

As I close out this chapter on rest, I want to quote Pastor John Gray as he encouraged men in the audience at Lakewood Church in 2015 by saying, "The woman is the 'rest' of you." Yes! When a man truly learns how to rest in the Father's rest, the right woman will be able to **help** him accomplish the work placed before him.

Also, I believe if you start to apply this principle of rest in your life, you will start seeing fruit like never before. I actually started with this step years ago, and I and the people around me have seen God do some amazing things that only He can get credit for. This is not about me at all but, rather, about a love so powerful that it brought a young man who was in the dark into His marvelous light. Because of accepting this lifestyle and following these principles myself, I can ecstatically say, "Now, I'm just waiting on my rib!"

Prayer for Rest

Father, simply teach me how to rest fully in You! You are so good and so patient with me. When I grow busy, or show signs of being a workaholic, help me find my peace in You. You are my Provider! Help me remember that. Remove the love of money from me as well. Thank You for sending Your Son to take away my sins and the sins of everyone in the world. In Jesus' name I pray. Amen.

Reflection Section

_____

_____

_____

_____

_____

_____

_____

_____

_____

_____

_____

_____

Part Two:
Meeting the Right One

"A guy and a girl can be just friends, but at one point or another, they will fall for each other ... Maybe temporarily, maybe at the wrong time, maybe too late, or maybe forever."

–Dave Matthews Band

Chapter 7
Boaz: A Completely Single Male

As I was writing this book, I really felt that I needed to share an example of someone other than Adam who had the characteristics of a completely single person. Then I was reminded of a study I once did on Boaz. A lot of women are told to look for their Boaz; however, after conversing with women on this subject, there still seems to be some misunderstanding of what "looking for their Boaz" really means, or what he would look like if he were standing in a woman's presence.

This is a brief description of the revelation I received on the subject. For the benefit of men and women alike, it will shed light on how a man should pursue a woman. Also, it will help men see what qualities they need to ask the Lord to instill in them so that each of them can be the man God intends for him to be—on the earth and for his future wife.

Boaz Was Completely Single!

In today's society, relating to the opposite sex, dating, or even courting for marriage can be challenging. With the world's demands for instant gratification, and the self-centered images of "the good life" that inundate popular culture, women and men avoid the "single"-minded thought of entering into a committed relationship.

So the question arises: What's the proper way to enter into a relationship? In the book of Ruth, the author shows some amazing insight on how a **completely single** man, Boaz, is supposed to relate to a potential spouse, Ruth. As we read through Ruth chapter 2, we will focus primarily on Boaz's pursuit.

> *There was a relative of Naomi's husband, a man of great wealth, of the family of Elimelech. His name was Boaz. So Ruth the Moabitess said to Naomi, "Please let me go to the field, and glean heads of grain after him in whose sight I may find favor."*
>
> *And she said to her, "Go, my daughter."*
>
> *Then she left, and went and gleaned in the field after the reapers. And she happened to come to the part of the field belonging to Boaz, who was of the family of Elimelech* (Ruth 2:1–3 NKJV).

Chapter 2 starts off with some very important information that I believe we rush through to get to the meat of the story. It tells us that Boaz is a kinsman-redeemer. The kinsman-redeemer was a male relative who, according to various laws of the Pentateuch, had the privilege or responsibility to act on behalf of a relative who was in trouble, danger, or need. The Hebrew term (**go el**) for kinsman-redeemer designates one who delivers or rescues (Genesis 48:16; Exodus 6:6), or redeems property or a person (Leviticus 27:9–25, 25:47–55).

What made Boaz a kinsman-redeemer? Scripture tells us that the family of Boaz was from the clan of Elimelech, which can be translated as "My God is King." This means that Boaz came from a family of royalty (spiritually); it also made Boaz a relative of Naomi on her husband's side by marriage. Therefore, Boaz had family ties to Ruth—he was a kinsman.

And as we shall see, Boaz was also a redeemer. In fact, in this story, he is a type and shadow of Christ—our kinsman-redeemer who takes our bad blood and restores us with His perfect blood. Furthermore, Boaz's name meant "strong and powerful," which were also qualities given to God our King. He was from a line of kings, and he walked in the glory of the heavenly King.

Now behold, Boaz came from Bethlehem, and said to the reapers, "The Lord be with you!"

And they answered him, "The Lord bless you!" (Ruth 2:4 NKJV)

In Ruth 2:4 Boaz, who was traveling from Bethlehem, enters the scene in the field that he owns and shows that he has respect for the "least of these." Boaz was upholding the Law set forth by God in Leviticus 19:9–10, which commands those who have fields to allow the poor to come in, work, and glean the leftovers:

> *When you reap the harvest of your land, you shall not wholly reap the corners of your field, nor shall you gather the gleanings of your harvest. And you shall not glean your vineyard, nor shall you gather every grape of your vineyard; you shall leave them for the poor and the stranger: I am the Lord your God.* (NKJV)

Some fields allowed up to thirty percent of the harvest to be left for the poor. One thing we see right away is that, even though Boaz was a powerful man, he still took the time to **recognize** and **bless** those who were at a lower social status. He is shown to have spiritual authority along with this status.

> *Then Boaz said to his servant who was in charge of the reapers, "Whose young woman is this?"*
>
> *So the servant who was in charge of the reapers answered and said, "It is the young Moabite woman who came back with Naomi from the country*

of Moab. And she said, 'Please let me glean and gather after the reapers among the sheaves.' So she came and has continued from morning until now, though she rested a little in the house. (Ruth 2:5–27 NKJV)

But after he blesses his workers, Boaz notices a particular woman, perhaps because she looks different from the others or seems to have potential. That is, Boaz sees Ruth, who is a Moabite (probably of darker complexion). So he asks one of his servants, "Whose young woman is this?"—in other words, "Wow, who is that?" Boaz falls in love at first sight. The servant explains to Boaz that Ruth is the daughter-in-law of Naomi, who followed after her from Moab. He tells his servant to bring her to him.

Then Boaz said to Ruth, "You will listen, my daughter, will you not? Do not go to glean in another field, nor go from here, but stay close by my young women. Let your eyes be on the field which they reap, and go after them. Have I not commanded the young men not to touch you? And when you are thirsty, go to the vessels and drink from what the young men have drawn." (Ruth 2:8–9 NKJV)

Boaz introduces himself and then proceeds to tell Ruth to glean in his field because it is safer. Also, if she gets thirsty, she can drink from the vessels that his men have drawn out of the ground. What Boaz is doing is giving Ruth **direction** by telling her that a certain job and place would suit her better. At the same time, he is also supplying **provision** and **security,** or **protection.** Boaz's men will now look after her, and he assures her that she will not be harmed. Gleaning in his field means that his people will look out for her, which also offers her **comfort**.

> *So she fell on her face, bowed down to the ground, and said to him, "Why have I found favor in your eyes, that you should take notice of me, since I am a foreigner?"* (Ruth 2:10 NKJV)

Ruth is overwhelmed by his kindness and asks Boaz why he is doing so much for her, showing her so much favor. This is very important because she is a foreigner, and to have this man protect her is a very big deal, especially because she is also poor. Ruth knows that Boaz is taking a risk to protect her—and that he also risks ridicule by his clan and family. But Boaz does not care. He is in love.

> *And Boaz answered and said to her, "It has been fully reported to me, all that you have done for your mother-in-law since the death of your husband, and how you have left your father and your mother and the land of your birth, and have come to a peo-*

ple whom you did not know before. The Lord repay your work, and a full reward be given you by the Lord God of Israel, under whose wings you have come for refuge."

Then she said, "Let me find favor in your sight, my lord; for you have comforted me, and have spoken kindly to your maidservant, though I am not like one of your maidservants." (Ruth 2:11–13 NKJV)

Boaz says he has heard about Ruth following her mother-in-law after the death of both of their husbands. You see, word spread about Ruth before Boaz ever laid eyes on her. Now he can put a face to a name. He studies her from a distance and then wants to show favor to her. From the background info Boaz has about Ruth, he can also see the traits of leadership and commitment that are embedded in her character.

After that he blesses her with the peace of God. Boaz has now introduced himself as her **male spiritual covering**, which she lacked due to the death of her husband. Boaz shows this even in the beginning of Ruth chapter 2, when he enters the field and blesses the harvesters. He is not afraid of being the covering, and he has confidence in the God he serves.

Now Boaz said to her at mealtime, "Come here,

and eat of the bread, and dip your piece of bread in the vinegar." So she sat beside the reapers, and he passed parched grain to her; and she ate and was satisfied, and kept some back. (Ruth 2:14 NKJV)

Now, at dinnertime, Boaz has invited Ruth in with the other harvesters to eat and to find rest. However, in verse 14, Boaz has Ruth dip bread into wine vinegar, which is very important in their culture. This simple act of dipping a piece of bread in the vinegar automatically elevates her to the position of second-highest person in the house. When this takes place, it is a direct sign that Boaz cares for her well-being and has a place for her at his table, even though she is a poor foreign woman. Boaz is willing to open his quarters, sacrifice his reputation, and provide **shelter** for Ruth. Because Ruth is obedient and under the provision of Boaz, she is blessed beyond measure.

And when she rose up to glean, Boaz commanded his young men, saying, "Let her glean even among the sheaves, and do not reproach her. Also let grain from the bundles fall purposely for her; leave it that she may glean, and do not rebuke her." (Ruth 2:15–16 NKJV)

Boaz commands the workers not only to allow her to glean, but also to leave good grain for her to glean. He tells them as well that if she comes back because they dropped some good grains, they should not rebuke her. Boaz is the man! He has dominion and knows how to use it for the woman he falls in love with.

> *So she gleaned in the field until evening, and beat out what she had gleaned, and it was about an ephah of barley. Then she took it up and went into the city, and her mother-in-law saw what she had gleaned.*
>
> *So she brought out and gave to her what she had kept back after she had been satisfied.*
>
> *And her mother-in-law said to her, "Where have you gleaned today? And where did you work? Blessed be the one who took notice of you."*
>
> *So she told her mother-in-law with whom she had worked, and said, "The man's name with whom I worked today is Boaz."* (Ruth 2:17–19 NKJV)

Ruth returns to Naomi with more than enough grain to feed them many times over. It is equal to the amount of a typical day's wages, which is unusual for the poor to gather in one day.

As Ruth 2:1 tells us, Boaz was "a man of great wealth" (NKJV). Theologian J. Vernon McGree suggests that this can also be interpreted to mean Boaz was a mighty man of war or a mighty man who understands the Law. We see all of this come together when Boaz, in chapter 4, follows the customs and laws of the day by redeeming Naomi's land and taking Ruth as his wife.

Below are some lessons that we can pick out from this story: Males should provide spiritual covering, direction (a vision for her), provision (such as financial), security, protection, comfort, and shelter. They should also be willing to elevate a future spouse to her rightful position beside them. If you cannot provide all of these things, it doesn't mean you stop looking. However, it means that you (males) must pray to God to give you insight on the areas in which you need strength.

One thing we must not overlook is that Boaz was an owner—he owned the field Ruth entered and gleaned in. This principle of ownership and personal benevolence is a mindset that sometimes gets lost under an impersonal government that seeks to assist millions of citizens. As men and women of Christ, we should continue to pray that we accept the authority given to us by Jesus and also walk in dominion as kings in the earth.

The example of Boaz is useful for young, single males looking for a future spouse, and for young, single females who want to know what to look for in a completely single male. One lesson is clear—Boaz was not looking for that perfect supermodel, as we males tend to do, but for someone with special potential who had character!

Reflection Section

Bonus: Only Read if You are Truely Becoming Completley Single

Chapter 8
ACE-ing Your Courtship

...and said, "For this reason a man shall leave his father and mother and be joined to his wife, and the two shall become one flesh"? So then, they are no longer two but one flesh. Therefore what God has joined together, let not man separate.

—Matthew 19:5–6 (NKJV)

Creating a Suitable Environment

Now that you have learned some of the principles to become #CompletelySingle, I think it's time to establish what it means to court a potential mate. The verb *court* is not found in the Bible; however there are principles sprinkled throughout the word of God to help in relating to the opposite sex in a godly way. If I could give a Christian (or believer of Jesus Christ) a definition for courting, it would be "developing a relationship with the opposite sex to see if God is leading them to an external union for eternal purposes, without destroying their walk as a disciple of Jesus Christ."

One reason I am cautious about using the term *dating*

is because the world has dragged this word through the dirt—and in general has corrupted biblical ways of interacting with people. In my experience, and from what I have heard when individuals date nowadays, it seems that people are mentally and physically testing out other individuals and treating them as if they were disposable objects. When one person is used up or seems *outdated*, he or she gets tossed back into the sea like a fish and we wait for the next catch to come along. It's truly sad. This pattern is harming a lot of couples before and after marriage, as divorce is at a staggering rate of fifty-plus percent.

How many of you remember taking tests in grade school, high school, or college? Now, how many of you remember not studying for those same tests? Brutal, right? A competent teacher would provide you enough information before the test so you could be successful. However, it is up to the student to study the material in order to ACE the test when given. If the student doesn't know or study the appropriate information at all, it will be tougher for that student to score a high grade on the exam.

I believe the same thing happens in relating to the op-posite sex. We fail the test because the world gives us bits and pieces of broken advice from broken people. We then try to take the test with this broken advice, and the opposite sex is harmed because inaccurate study material was used. The funny thing is, the Bible gives us great advice for relating not only to the opposite sex but to the same gender as well.

Unfortunately, we seem unaware that this information is available, or we don't believe it will be beneficial to our current relationship. We just have to look at the current mindset and statistics about relationships to see which direction our society is headed. But God wants to set you up for success! I believe if we use the Bible and its wisdom, fewer feelings would be hurt and people would know how to relate more effectively. This would create a suitable environment not only for our generation but also for the generations to come.

It is with this mindset that I write this last section for you. Some close friends who said I should write a book on relationships nudged me to include this subject as well. So I have studied these subjects for myself. I have asked close friends and other couples about things that have brought success to their relationships before they tied the knot. Also, I asked where they thought they made mistakes.

Below is the result of my investigation—a comprehensive list developed through my sphere of influences, though there may well be a few things you wish to add.

My intent is to help you set a strong foundation for your current and future relationships. So here it is—the six principles in "ACE"-ing your courtship:

rACE

I believe the topic of race is one of the most important when it comes to relating to the opposite sex today. We live in a diverse world, but race splits families apart and destroys potential relationships. I want to address it first from a biblical standpoint.

What do you see? You know, there is a popular saying in our world today that perception is everything. I believe this statement is partly true; however, a follow-up question would be: Through which eyes are you looking? This is the deeper matter! To say that I don't see color when I look at people would be a lie, but I can say God has given me, and continues to give me, His eyes because I prayed for them. Of course I can see color—because I have cones in my eyes that make me see it.

When I read the word of God, I see Jesus put Himself on a cross not for me alone, an African American. Even though I truly believe that if I were the last person on earth, He still would have died for me—because He is just that awesome! I know that He died for you, too. No matter your race, culture, or nationality, He died for you.

And the most wonderful news of all is that despite your religious beliefs, dogmas, or practices, Jesus still died for you. He loved you so much that He didn't care if you were going to accept Him or not. He died anyway, which meant you were already accepted. He did all the hard work for you. We don't have to perform for His love or acceptance, unlike what other religions teach. He is the only way back to God the Father, and that's why we accept Jesus (John 14:6).

So if Jesus didn't care what race, culture, or nationality we come from, why should we care? Keep in mind that the principles to ACE-ing your courtship are geared toward individuals who have already taken the first courageous step and accepted Jesus Christ as their personal Savior. I believe that's the only way these principles can truly be practiced, applied, and sustained throughout your life.

For instance, the Bible lays out why we shouldn't care about race, especially in our relationships, in Galatians 3:26–28. I absolutely love these verses because they get us away from looking at our differences, although differences can be good when used to advance the kingdom of God. We tend to use these verses to tear each other apart and not be unified. However, we have to be aware that this is one of the tactics that the enemy uses to destroy relationships. Galatians 3:26–28 reads,

*"For you are all sons of God through faith in Christ Jesus. For as many of you as were baptized into Christ have put on Christ. There is neither **Jew nor Greek**, there is neither slave nor free, there is neither male nor female; for you are all one in Christ Jesus"* (NKJV).

Paul was telling us that when we accept Christ as our Lord and Savior, the Father sees us as His Son. Why? Because we have been spiritually baptized in Christ, so God doesn't see our sins anymore; rather, He sees His Son's blood sacrifice, which is enough to save us from hell. Paul went on to say that there is neither Jew nor Greek, which were races of people who did not see eye to eye in biblical times. They had their biases and differences, just as certain races do today.

My friends, I said all of this because when we enter into the kingdom of God, our focus must be on Jesus. When we are seeking a relationship with the opposite sex, our focus must be on Jesus, not on the color of the other person's skin, or his or her nationality. If the person is a believer and follower of Jesus Christ who is **truly single**, and if you are attracted to him or her, you should pursue a relationship together. Yes, this may violate the family traditions of marrying inside your race; however, the kingdom of God is bigger than any race—just remember that! We are all sons of God.

fACE

The second principle to ACE-ing your courtship is to bring your face in His. To what am I referring? Seeking the face of God, which puts you right into His kingdom. Matthew 6:33 says, *"But seek first the **kingdom of God** and His righteousness, and all these things shall be added to you"* (NKJV). The revelation of the kingdom is what we are after, and this will be pivotal to your courtship. Let me explain.

The lust for autonomy is one of the biggest struggles we have. This means we must contend with the idea of governing ourselves; we must battle against our tendency toward self-rule and a strong sense of independence. Since we are made in the image of God, we sometimes act as if we're gods ourselves. We think we can make better decisions than God Himself, don't we? We sometimes wonder why He keeps us away from certain individuals, or we rush into a relationship—taking our life in our own hands to end up right on our face. Then we have the audacity to blame God for those relationships.

But let me bring some truth to the forefront here and quote E. Jay O'Keefe, who says, "God is good and He has our best interest in mind." The faulty reasoning that we can do things better than God could leads to being oppressed by a spirit of anger and discontentment. On the flip side, we have this great opportunity to surrender all of our desires to God and seek His kingdom, especially in the area of finding and pursuing a mate.

So what exactly do we need to be seeking in the kingdom of God? Romans 14:17 explains that *"the kingdom of God is not eating and drinking, but **righteousness** and **peace** and **joy** in the Holy Spirit"* (NKJV). Take note of these qualities, which are needed to achieve our main goal—not to find the right person but, rather, to become the right person for the person we are looking for.

Do you exude righteousness? In other words, is it self-evident that you are living an equitable and holy life before God? You see, the world will know you by your fruit and by what we call the fruit of the Spirit. Are you producing the fruit of the Spirit or, instead, the fruit of the flesh? The fruit of the flesh are found in Galatians 5:19–21: *"Now the works of the flesh are evident, which are: adultery, fornication, uncleanness, lewdness, idolatry, sorcery, hatred, contentions, jealousies, outbursts of wrath, selfish ambitions, dissensions, heresies, envy, murders, drunkenness, revelries, and the like..."* (NKJV).

Really, take some time here and meditate on how you are living. You might be married, courting, or seeking singleness. Regardless, meditating on your lifestyle and placing holiness before the flesh are essential to living in peace.

Are you peaceful with your neighbor? Living a life of prosperity does not just mean financially, although some ministries focus their congregations in that direction, but also with prosperity in your health and in your relationships with others—especially your neighbors. Romans 12:18 instructs, *"If it is possible, as much as depends on you, live peaceably with all men"* (NKJV). Hebrews 12:14–15 adds, *"Pursue peace with all people, and holiness, without which no one will see the Lord: looking carefully lest anyone fall short of the grace of God; lest any root of bitterness springing up cause trouble, and by this many become defiled..."* (NKJV).

Very simply, learn to live in peace and learn how to handle offenses. Bitterness can take root and destroy your relationships, especially with the person you are courting. If there's something bothering you, talk about it and bring it out into the open. Communication is the key. Learning how to settle conflicts sooner rather than later will be a great foundation for your relationships. And at all times, remember to speak life! (See Proverbs 11:25.)

Lastly, do you have an unspeakable joy that only heaven can offer? Ask yourself whether you are a cheerful, happy person who is a delight to be around. Can you truly claim, "The joy of the Lord is my strength"? A lot of couples I have been around say, "I am not happy." As my father explained to me, your partner will always fail in trying to make you happy because earthly happiness is a bottomless pit of an emotion. We should earnestly seek the joy of the Lord in everything we do—and not try to find our identity in how happy our partner makes us, because that will soon go away.

Before you go out and pursue a mate, you need to first learn how to pursue God and receive all that He has for you. You want to develop character traits that can withstand the strains of any relationship between the opposite sexes. **And instead of praying for the right person, focus first on ensuring that you are a righteous (not self-righteous) person in the sight of God—on being peaceful and having your joy in the Lord.** This and the other fruits of the Spirit found in Galatians 5:22–23a develop the characteristics that encourage change in your courtship partner. Therefore, once you surrender and seek His kingdom, the discontentment in seeking happiness from people and your courtship partner is a problem that becomes more and more a non-issue.

pACE

Now, if you are lucky and recently got out of the "friend zone," this next principle is especially for you. The word *pace* is tough for a lot of people, young and old, because they are eager to jump right into a relationship. I believe the modern-day vernacular is that the person is "hungry." I remember struggling with this all the way up to my late twenties.

So, what do it mean to pace yourself? Once you finally enter into a relationship, the tendency is to spend an abnormal about of time with the person you are trying to court. My suggestion is to slow down.

For me, the problem was talking on the phone and texting all the time. I remember girls would tell me that they did not like talking on the phone so much before really getting to know me; however, for some reason, we would end up being on the phone for hours. A couple of years ago, I was on the phone for about five hours with a young lady who, when she realized the time, said "Oh, no!" And "oh, no!" is right.

We have to pace ourselves in spending time with the one we are courting. Texting should be limited as well. Seven or eight hours of texting was nothing for me at one point. However, I realized that the young ladies were becoming idols. I was manipulating them, and I lost sight of my first love, which was and is God.

Revelation 2:4 stares at me every time I read it: *"Nevertheless I have this against you, that you have left your first love"* (NKJV). God has to be number one, period. If your relationship is taking your time away from God—whether it's personal worship time at home, corporate worship time at church, or your study of the scriptures—I would second-guess that relationship and take a break from seeing each other. Another red flag is if the person distracts you from your work or your studies at your school. I remember in my senior year of high school, my basketball coach used to preach to my teammates and me, "If the girl ain't paying your school bills, you shouldn't be spending that much time with her right now."

You want to strive to develop a healthy friendship first and foremost because otherwise, you can get all emotionally tied into the person and have an unhealthy intimacy. The faster you fall for someone, the faster you will fall out of "like" for the same person. Guys and gals, taking it slow is not a bad idea.

Our goal here is to get to know the person. One of the words in the Old Testament that we see for relationship is *yada*. Now, you might have heard this word repeatedly quoted on the popular television series *Seinfeld*, but that is not the context in which we see this word in the Bible. As Kevin Dedmon of Bethel Church has explained, the biblical *yada* has a very deep meaning. Its root meaning is "to know"; however, it encompasses several other meanings that we can apply to our current relationships, before and after marriage.

1. **To know someone in complete detail.** This means to study, analyze, or investigate something or someone until you know the thing or person completely, just as Boaz did with Ruth. Study the person's behavior with his or her friends, parents, and small groups, and with those less fortunate.

2. **To know something technically.** This is to know how something works in a functional sense. What motivates this person? What excites this person or makes him or her sad or upset? What makes the person tick? You must learn these things!

3. **To know God by personal experience.** Is the person you are courting saved by Jesus Christ? Has this person accepted what Jesus did on the cross for him or her? How is the person's relationship with God? Is he or she bearing (spiritual) fruit? (Galatians 5:22–23a)

4. **Have a face-to-face encounter.** You can't date a person online (i.e., ChristianMingle, Facebook, Instagram, Twitter) or via text messages for the rest of your life. You need to have a face-to-face interaction with him or her. See the person for the attributes and characteristics he or she represents. This is also relevant to God Himself. To experience the fullness of His love, forgiveness, power, grace, mercy, and healing, you have to meet with Him on a regular basis.

5. **To know someone sexually.** This was only listed for the purposes of defining *yada* completely. However, biblical sex is considered a gift given to married couples. If you don't have meanings 1 to 4 down, it will be difficult and close to impossible to thrive sexually with your spouse in the long run. Again, this is for after you are legally married, not just engaged.

Now you have learned what *yada* means. This is why we teach singles to focus heavily on pacing themselves and getting to know the other person. If you feel rushed by the person to do things—even to get married—then the flesh, not the Spirit, is leading that person! 1 Corinthians 13:4 starts off by saying, *"Love is patient, love is kind"* (NIV). The New King James translation phrases this as *"Love suffers long."* A friend of mine really challenged me, as I was growing in my understanding that I had a broken mindset toward women, to substitute my name in place of *love* every time I read this passage. So it would read, "Damien is patient, Damien is kind…" Could you say you are (or were) patient when pursuing the opposite sex? Let's be truthful here!

Here are a few helpful tips for pacing yourself with your courtship partner:

- Remember, it's not the quantity of time spent together, in the beginning, but the quality of time.

- Try to set boundaries in talking on the phone and texting. For example, avoid contacting the person after 11 p.m. by phone or text.

- Limit phone and text time in general (to no more than two to three hours a day, for instance).

- Limit your time hanging out only with each other, especially in the beginning. Hang out with your church members, family, or small group. Make sure these groups are truly holding you both accountable!

- Remember that you don't have to see each other every day. Once or twice a week, in the very beginning, is a great place to start.

Proverbs 4:23 says, *"Above all else, guard your heart, for everything you do flows from it"* (NIV). God really wants to protect you from getting hurt or, worse, ending up in bondage, as we saw in chapter 4. Therefore, we should seek to guard and protect our hearts. Adhering to boundaries set up by both parties so you can one day enter into your marriage without shame or guilt does this. (Please refer to chapter 4 for more suggested boundaries.)

Finally, I was privileged to speak at a conference in 2014 called "Kingdom Relationships," which is where I announced I was writing this book for singles. The facilitator sent me the ten questions below. I believe every couple should really meditate on these together as they seek the Holy Spirit in moving forward with their relationship.

Ten ways to know if you're unequally yoked in your relationship

1. If the person with whom you are in a relationship starts to see that you are being clingy, does he or she enjoy it or, instead, try to draw your attention and focus toward God?

2. Have you seen yourself sinning more toward God now than before? Take counsel from a spiritually

mature couple to help determine this, and put a pause to the relationship if needed.

3. How often does the person with whom you are in a relationship initiate spiritual things—prayer, devotion, Bible study, godly conversation, and witnessing to other believers? When you initiate these godly things, what is the other person's attitude or response?

4. Are there areas in your life in which you know you could not have grown without the spiritual advice of the other person in your relationship? Is this person helping you to grow?

5. Involve outsiders to your relationship. Ask four of your closest spiritual friends if they believe your walk with God has improved or declined since being in the relationship.

6. Ask the same four people if your purpose has been hindered or advanced since being in the relationship.

7. Go to the two closest friends of the person with whom you are in a relationship and ask: In what ways has your relationship hindered or blessed their friend spiritually?

8. What kind of example has your relationship set in the church? If no one knows, then that could be a sign in itself. If you are not able to answer, then you are probably ashamed and not living out what the Bible says.

9. Can you give five biblical reasons why you know the person you are with has truly been born again?

10. If the person with whom you're in a relationship knew that your relationship were being hindered, do they love God to step away for a season—or forever—to allow you to restore your relationship with Christ?

If you can't answer "yes" or "no" to this question, then you need to have a serious conversation with your partner about moving forward or, perhaps, taking a break from seeing each other.

spACE

Joshua Harris's book *Boy Meets Girl* is a great reference in courting a mate. Here is a quote from his book in which he deals with the topic of space:

> The amount of space your friendship occupies in your life will also grow over time. In the beginning, be careful that it doesn't crowd out the

relationships with friends and families. Don't be threatened by other relationships the other person has. Make room for each other. Don't try to monopolize each other's time. Remember that premature exclusivity in your courtship can cause both of you to depend on it more than is wise. Be faithful to your current friendships and responsibilities. As the relationship progresses, you'll make more and more space for each other, but this should happen slowly and be done cautiously.

I can tell you from my own life that I have struggled at times to deal with what Mr. Harris has so eloquently laid out for us. As I meditate on the topic, I believe one of the main areas that affect "space," or the lack thereof, is insecurity. If we are transparent here, most of us deal with, or have dealt with, insecurities.

So, what are some insecurities that may affect our relationships, friendships, and courtships?

- Current living situation

- Financial position

- Education

- Relationship with our families

- Physical appearance

- Hygiene

- Personality traits (introvert or extrovert)

- Hidden addictions

- Abuse

- Time away from the relationship scene

- Unsuccessful relationships in the past

- Relationship with God

You may be able to relate to some or even all of these potential insecurities; however, the psalmist gives us a great affirmation in Psalm 139:14: *"I will praise You, for I am fearfully and wonderfully made..."* (NKJV). Isaiah 43:1 tells us that He names us. Jeremiah 1:5 asserts that before we were born in the womb, He knew us. And Jesus proclaimed, according to Luke 12:7, that the very hairs on our heads are numbered. I just love the word of God because it confirms that we are here for a purpose and that we can put all of our security not in ourselves, but in Jesus Christ. What I know to be true is that He is all the truth we need to be set free!

Do not let insecurities inflict a toll on your current

relationships as you court your mate. Give each other space! You will have plenty of time to be exclusive when you are married. So enjoy life and respect past **godly**—not ungodly—relationships that your partner has worked so hard to develop. Because the fact is, those relationships are what shaped him or her into the person you ultimately fell for.

Also, do not let your insecurities or fears of being alone and not in a relationship keep you in a bad relationship. In some cases this is what we call *missionary dating*, and we see it all the time: women will attempt to change their man. They would try to decorate or upgrade their man, making him (and themselves) look better to everyone than they truly are. This puts unwanted expectations on the man, trying to turn him into a person he is not or doesn't desire to become. Eventually, his true character will surface. **Women, believe me when I tell you that you can't upgrade his character!**

And men, we like to fix women, don't we? Men sometimes offer broken women outlandish dreams with no clear plan, which they cannot deliver. A man will also sometimes manipulate the woman, or try to control her, to create a sense of dependency so she will feel inadequate without him. This is wrong and can cause women years of grief and pain.

Don't think you have to be with somebody for the person to change or so you can "fix" him or her. This is one of the biggest mistakes I see in relationships today. Now, I am not saying that you should be perfect or enter into a relationship perfect. However, you need to strive to use these principles laid out in this book to become the best person you can be—to be single, holy, and set apart as God is calling you to be.

People just don't want to wait on the process, and then they try to blame heaven for all of their disobedience. You are not God. Oftentimes, you can become an idol or even a god to the other person in your relationship, in which case your presence usually prevents him or her from really receiving the necessary healing and deliverance. God clearly tells Moses in Exodus 20:3, *"You shall have no other gods before Me"* (NKJV). Very plainly, you are not God— so get out of the way!

Space may even mean separation from the individual for some time—or permanently!

Pray this short prayer: "God, show me if this person is in my life for a **season**, for a **reason,** or for **treason. Amen!**"

You know, what I have learned over the years is that God sometimes orchestrates people to come into our lives seasonally. However, just like with the seasons, we try to hold on to these people way too long. These individuals usually highlight strengths and weakness in our relational style that will help us as we grow in the Lord. Yet, again, we tend to hold on too long. I suggest letting go of these seasonal blessings and just praying for them from a distance. If God wants you back together, whether as a friend or as a potential mate, He is fully capable of parading you two in front of each other again. Is the person I'm courting only a seasonal relationship for my growth?

On the other hand, you can readily discern what it looks like for a person to be in your life for a reason. Whether it is your friend or your courtship partner, this relationship is fruit-bearing in nature, and God's kingdom is being advanced. Remember, though, that there can also be relationships God allows in your life to show your heart. Just be vigilant, prayerful in all your relationships, and attentive to what God is saying.

Lastly, I say "for treason" because the enemy will try to place people in your life to try to kill your relationship with the sovereign God. This person takes your time away from God and doesn't apologize for it, either. The enemy wants to try to overthrow the government of God's kingdom, which He wants to establish through our relationships with other believers and, more importantly, our relationship with Him. Therefore, the enemy will send counterfeits to divert you from your destiny so that you might marry the wrong person.

We must be aware of the enemy's schemes here. God has to be your number one. In your current relationship, is there more disunity than true unity? Jesus calls us to be unified, so this answer is a big hint as to whether your relationship is going to work.

I leave you with Proverbs 3:5–6, which tells us, *"Trust in the Lord with all your heart, and lean not on your own understanding; in all your ways acknowledge Him, and He shall direct your paths"* (NKJV). Focus more on Christ during your relationship, putting your full trust in Him. You will never go wrong with that advice—never!

plACE

Now that you guys are hanging out more and more with each other, it is very important to review every **place** you go. The key word here is *intentionality.* "What are my intentions today or tonight? Why are we going here, and who is going to be there to keep us accountable?" You can go back and read my close call in chapter 4 to see what I mean about place and intentionality. My intentions were not pure.

I call this the "How Far" struggle. You know what I am

talking about—your mental conversation goes something like, "How far can I go with this person before it is considered sin?" Even thinking this can turn into sin because you are then fantasizing about what you are going to do to the other person.

There are two scriptures in particular I go to when I get the urge to fall back into the "How Far" struggle. The first is 2 Timothy 2:22: *"Flee also youthful lusts; but pursue righteousness, faith, love, peace with those who call on the Lord out of a pure heart"* (NKJV). The other is 1 Corinthians 6:18: *"Flee sexual immorality. Every sin that a man does is outside the body, but he who commits sexual immorality sins against his own body"* (NKJV). We see that both of these scriptures begin with the word *flee*, which in the original text can mean "to run away."

That's right—I am giving you permission literally to throw on your shoes and run as fast as you can from any spiritually and physically hazardous situation you stumble into. I have seen and heard about people who did not run, and now they have unwanted "baby mama" or "baby daddy" drama that they will have to deal with for at least the next eighteen years. This is so sad to me, and I know God does not want to put more on you than you can bear. However, we place ourselves in situations and then blame God for not offering grace. Grace covers mistakes, not pure disobedience. We can't expect God to go against His own words.

With this in mind, start your relationship by hanging out primarily with your biblical community and your small group members. At least you will have several eyes keeping you accountable. You can also go out on dates in which you volunteer together. Then you can see how the person interacts with others in various situations, and your focus will be more on serving than on being tempted with lust.

Eventually, you are going to be alone one-on-one, which is also important. But do this prayerfully during the early stages as you build into your relationship certain boundaries that will keep you from creating situations to fall. It's about maturing together in Christ despite our natural feelings. Now, if you are studying the Word of God with your courtship partner, doing Bible studies is a great place to sharpen each other and keeping Him first.

So I believe you have gotten the point. You and your courtship partner should always be aware of the places you are going and make sure that you are not alone for long periods of time with the door closed. Trust me it is hard to resist the temptation no matter how strong you think you might be.

grACE

I hear from more and more couples that either the

male or the female, if not both, compares his or her current mate to previous relationships. This is a big no-no! Please, if you want this relationship to work at all, refrain from such comparisons. Your potential husband or wife is not your ex! Again—he or she is not your ex! So stop thinking and acting otherwise.

One of my pastors has noted that "comparison is the enemy of contentment"; it is the bed of discontentment. This person looks different, unless you start courting his or her twin brother or sister—which would be kind of scary! I would probably have to write a whole new book on that subject alone. But this person also smells different, has a different height, speaks differently, and has a different background and family tree. So we can all agree that the person you are now seeing and talking to **is not your ex!**

Given this, your potential husband or wife is going to make his or her own mistakes. He or she probably will do things that will make you upset once in a while, as you are learning who this person really is behind the scenes. However, if you are both single—and I hope you both are reading this book to become #CompletelySingle—then you may have become aware of the things the enemy wants to do to destroy your relationship. Now you are going to apply this last word to your relationship: That word is **grace.** As writer Wayne Jackson explains, *grace* (**charis**) is found in the New Testament 156 times, and it means favor, benefit, gift, joy, worthy, liberality, or the divine influence on the heart.

One thing we must come to understand is that we can't truly offer grace to another person if we have never received the grace first given to us by God when He sent His son Jesus to die on the cross for our sins. You see, grace is a concept created by God and given by God. John 3:16 tells us about this grace: *"For God so loved the world that He gave His only begotten Son, that whoever believes in Him should not perish but have everlasting life"* (NKJV). That is the true definition of *grace*.

God made every human to be worthy of life, which we don't deserve. Let that sink in for a second. Now let's apply this concept to our current and future relationships: we always want to pray for godly discernment in every relationship we enter.

I am not saying you ought to allow people to use and manipulate you. However, you ought to apply the grace method and not expect your partner to knock a home run out of the park every single time when you are in the process of getting to know each other. Forgive quickly and then move on within the relationship. And the reason we can forgive is because He first forgave us (Ephesians 4:32). *SELAH.*

Reflection Section

_____

_____

_____

_____

_____

_____

_____

_____

_____

_____

_____

_____

_____

Sneak Peek

We have come to the end of this book, and I really enjoyed our time together. I hope you received a few nuggets you can apply to your life, your current relationships, and may even share within your circle of influence.

Finally, I wanted to leave you with a story that became one of the most memorable and popular *Thoughts From The Box* of 2014. *Thoughts From The Box* is a monthly devotional I write to encourage, educate, and inspire people to be the best they can be. This is one way God continues to minister to me every month, and I give the devotional away free to those on my email list. This particular *Thought* dealt with the subject of relationships and can be a seedbed for you to start seeing relationships in a new light. This is my gift to you, as it is a sneak preview. It will be featured in my next thirty-one-day devotional book! Enjoy…

Out-Serve Him

The following account is a very sensitive subject to me. It's difficult to share something so personal. However, I felt led to write about this personal experience to help free one or more of my readers from their present and/or future relationships.

If you've taken the time to read one of my posts over the last four years, you have noticed I love writing about my family. Family is extremely important to me, personally, and it is the backbone of who we are as the Nashes.

We all know, however, that even though family is very important, and the structure of biblical families is being threatened daily, that families still have their own opportunities, or what the world calls "issues." The reason I say "opportunities" is because every issue can really be looked upon as an opportunity for God to go to work and get the glory.

In saying this, I want to bring you into my world—actually, into my home a little bit—and recount a dispute that my former womb-mate, and now my roommate, once had:

I am a twin. (We turned thirty in February of 2014.) Some of you know that my twin's name is Julien. Well, what some of you don't know is that Julien despises dirty dishes. And that's putting it mildly. He frequently makes this appeal: "Dawg, keep the common areas clean." And that definitely includes the kitchen, especially the sink area. So what did I do? Very simply, I left dishes out all the time.

One day after coming home from a trip, I saw that the kitchen was spotless. I was a little hungry, so I put my bags down and returned to the kitchen to start cooking. However, something was wrong. I could not find any pots or pans that I was used to cooking with.

I searched and searched, and I found nothing. Then I had a weird feeling, so I went in the garage and—guess what? I found that Julien had put **all** of the dirty dishes I had used before my trip (about four days earlier) in the garage.

To say I was mad is an understatement. I fussed and yelled and **dared** him to do it again. Have you ever been so mad with someone that you dared them to cross that line? Who can relate? I can just see some of you shaking your heads right now.

Okay, calm down. It is going to be all right— but guess what? He did it again. Then I went to God, still mad and upset, and asked Him what I should do to Julien. God responded, "Out-serve him." What? What does that mean, "Out-serve him"?

"God, I mean how can I get him back or hurt him?" I tried to reason with the Lord. God had spoken, however, so I knew I must obey.

I told myself that I was going to try to do better by

cleaning everyone's dishes, including the ones used by Julien and my other roommates. I remember one or two instances of "I 'preciate ya" from my other room-mates, but I don't remember Julien saying anything. Then, I remember, one day I forgot again to clean the dishes, and guess what? This boy put all my dishes in the garage again.

Julien was gone that time, so I phoned him, and I yelled and I screamed. This time I wanted to force a chore onto him. "I don't like the floor dirty!" I said. "So if I have to do the dishes, you have to sweep!"

Do you think that worked?

The next day the floor was still dirty, and I literally lost it. You cannot imagine what I did next.

I took a permanent marker and wrote on the laundry room wall: "JULIEN SWEEP THE FLOOR!" with three big arrows pointing to the ground. Why the laundry room? Well, he walks through the laundry room every day after putting his trailer up, when he comes home from cutting yards. That day, my brother came home and walked right past the wall but was not affected by it at all. God convicted me and said, "Why would you do that?"

This conviction was painful, yet necessary. My writing

did not even stay on the wall for a full twenty-four hours before I painted over it. Then God said, "Didn't I tell you to out-serve him?" So you know what? I swept the floor—and made sure the dishes were clean that day as well.

Over the next few weeks and months, I tried my best to make sure the dishes were clean. As soon as I got off of work, I tried my best to wash the dishes. It was tough, and I probably missed a couple of days but it was apparent that the kitchen was staying clean. I would even chant to myself, "Out-serve him."

One night I was half-asleep when I heard the dishes being washed. After fully drifting off, I jumped up and said, "Shoot, I forgot to wash my dishes!"

I bolted downstairs. Seeing that the kitchen was clean, I dashed straight to the garage, thinking all my dishes were probably stacked back on the shelves. So I opened the door to the garage briskly, and guess what I found? No dishes! I smiled slightly. "That boy washed my dishes."

And Julien had actually washed my dishes. God's lessons are so funny, and He is always right.

Do you know what the word *family* means? The root word is **familia,** and it means "to serve." What God has taught me from this experience is that, as a leader and child in the kingdom or family of God, I am called to serve no matter what my gender or background.

Family, we are called to serve. We can't expect people to change before we start loving them; we must first focus on the change inside ourselves.

Jesus tells us in Matthew 22:39 that *"the second [most important commandment] is like it: 'Love your neighbor as yourself'"* (NIV). The problem was not Julien—it was me. I did not truly love myself; therefore, I was unable to love my brother.

Take this into your personal relationships. Are you having petty arguments because of unmet expectations from your spouse, friends, or the person you are courting? Think about it: Are your expectations unreachable? How can someone make you happy if you're not happy yourself? See, your joy comes from the Lord. It's not the job of others to keep you happy but, rather, to serve you and help you achieve your purpose in life while you are doing the same for them.

Here's some advice you can take away from all of this: I'm learning not to expect anything, which is helping me learn how to appreciate everything—even the smallest of deeds.

And I know what you're asking. Has Julien put my dishes in the garage since? I can honestly say, "Nope!"

Prayer

Father, thank You for Your example of not holding a grudge against Your children. May we learn how to love as You do and have mercy on those who may never change. In Jesus' name I pray. Amen.

Blessings!

By Damien K. H. Nash
Founder/CEO TNG Publishings, LLC

Reflection Section

_____

_____

_____

_____

_____

_____

_____

_____

_____

_____

_____

_____

References

Print Sources

Bevere, John. *The Holy Spirit: An Introduction*. Palmer Lake, CO: Messenger International, 2013. Print.

Eckhardt, John. *Deliverance and Spiritual Warfare Manual*. Lake Mary: Charisma House, 2014. Print.

Harris, Joshua. *Boy Meets Girl: Say Hello to Courtship*. Sisters, OR: Multnomah, 2000. Print.

Hendrickson, Mark. *Supernatural Provision Where God Guides, He Provides*. Shippensburg: Destiny Image, 2011. Print.

McGee, J. Vernon. *Thru the Bible. Vol. 1*. Nashville: T. Nelson, 1982. Print.

Munroe, Myles. *Understanding Your Place in God's Kingdom: Your Original Purpose for Existence*. Shippensburg: Destiny Image, 2011. Print.

Nash, Damien K. H. *Thoughts From The Box: 31 Day Devotional*. Conyers: TNG Publishing, 2013. Print.

O'Keefe, E. Jay. *Biblical Economics:* Beginning at Square One. Amarillo, TX: Westcliff, 2006. Print.

Sheets, Dutch. *The Beginner's Guide to Intercessory Prayer.* Ventura, CA: Gospel Light, 2004. Print.

Sherrer, Quin, and Ruthanne Garlock. *A Woman's Guide to Breaking Bondages.* Ann Arbor, Mich.: Vine, 1994. Print.

Strong, James. *The New Strong's Exhaustive Concordance of the Bible: With Main Concordance, Appendix to the Main Concordance, Topical Index to the Bible, Dictionary of the Hebrew Bible, Dictionary of the Greek Testament.* Nashville: T. Nelson, 1996. Print.

Electronic Sources

Bible Gateway. Web. Accessed 13 Nov. 2014–5 Feb. 2015.
https://www.biblegateway.com

Brooks, Gerald. "The Holy Spirit." 5 Oct. 2014. Online video clip. Accessed 29 Nov. 2014.

"Cultivate" Def. 5. *Dictionary.com.* Dictionary.com. Web. Accessed 25 Oct. 2007.
http://dictionary.reference.com/browse/cultivate?s=t

Dedmon, Kevin. "Yada." *Bethel.* Bethel, 2015. Web. Accessed 6 Jan. 2015.
http://www.ibethel.org/articles/2007/09/01/yada-yada-yada

Family Foundations International. *Ancient Paths with Craig Hill.* 2013. Web. Accessed 24 April 2014. https://www.craighill.org/

Goodreads. "C. G. Jung Quotes." *Goodreads.com.* Goodreads. Web. Accessed 3 May 2015. http://www.goodreads.com/author/ quotes/38285.C_G_Jung

Goodreads. "Dave Matthews Band Quotes." *Goodreads.com.* Goodreads. Web. Accessed 3 May 2015. http://www.goodreads.com/author/quotes/282969. Dave_Matthews_Band

Goodreads. "Elizabeth Gilbert Quotes." *Goodreads. com.* Goodreads. Web. Accessed 3 May 2015. http://www.goodreads.com/author/quotes/11679. Elizabeth_Gilbert

Goodreads. "Will Rogers Quotes." *Goodreads.com.* Goodreads. Web. Accessed 3 May 2015. http://www.goodreads.com/author/quotes/132444. Will_Rogers

Ingram, Chip. "This Is War ... Invisible War: The Ministry of Deliverance." *Living on the Edge.* Living on the Edge, 2014. Online video clips. Accessed 30 Dec. 2014. http://livingontheedge.org/group-studies/browse-all-studies/invisible-war

Jackson, Wayne. "The True Meaning of Grace." *Christian Courier.* Christian Courier. Web. Accessed 3 May 2015.
https://www.christiancourier.com/articles/1279-true-meaning-of-grace-the

Jeremiah, David. "Slaying the Giant of Loneliness." Online video clip. YouTube, 1 Dec. 2011. Web. Accessed 24 April 2014.
https://www.youtube.com/watch?v=5RSMzUsZolI

Lighthouseproject. "The Importance of Rest." Online video clip. YouTube, 5 Jan. 2010. Web. Accessed 12 Jan. 2015.
https://www.youtube.com/watch?v=nvkE4PyVZrs

Monroe, Myles. "Kingdom Keys to Successful Relationships." Online video clip. YouTube, 24 Aug. 2011. Web. Accessed 22 Nov. 2014.
http://www.youtube.com/watch?v=1Vny0DqwDcg

Stanley, Andy. "The Right Person Myth." Online video clip. The New Rules for Love, Sex & Dating. *North Point Community Church.* North Point Ministries, 1 May 2011. Web. Accessed 7 May 2015.
http://northpoint.org/messages/the-new-rules-for-love-sex-and-dating/the-right-person-myth

"Treason" Def. 1–3. *Dictionary.com*. Dictionary.com.
Web. Accessed 1 April 2015.
http://dictionary.reference.com/browse/treason?s=t

"What Is a Kinsman Redeemer?" *GotQuestions.org*.
Got Questions Ministries. Web. Accessed 27 Dec.
2014.
http://www.gotquestions.org/kinsman-redeemer.html

"Yoke, n." Def. 1. *Dictionary.com*. Dictionary.com.
Web. Accessed 19 Dec. 2014.
http://dictionary.reference.com/browse/yoke?s=t

About the Author

A college professor once told Damien K. H. Nash that he had among the worst writing ability she had ever encountered. Nash did not accept this label, and he took her comment as a challenge. Now, more than seven years later, he is the founder of TNG Publishings, a full-service publishing company.

Nash received a BA degree in Business Administration and an MBA from Bellarmine University, where he played college basketball, receiving the Coaches' Award his freshman year. He currently holds the position of coach for the leaders within his church's young adult ministry, called Fusion, in Norcross, GA.

Damien Nash is also a national speaker. He has presented at churches, businesses, schools, workshops, and conferences. Nash is the author of *How to Load Your Truck and Thoughts From The Box: 31 Day Devotional.* He also co-authored, directed, and executive-produced *Big Box, Little Box: How One Little Box Finds His Way* and *The Forecast Calls for Potential Rain*, a children's book series and animated film.

www.completelysingle.com

46020483R00134